Presented To:

_____

From:

_____

Date:

_____

GOD, YOU'VE GOT MAIL!

GOD, YOU'VE GOT MAIL!

15 Keys to Abundant Provision

Danette Joy Crawford

DESTINY IMAGE® PUBLISHERS, INC.
P.O. Box 310, Shippensburg, PA 17257-0310
"Promoting Inspired Lives."

This book and all other Destiny Image, Revival Press, MercyPlace, Fresh Bread, Destiny Image Fiction, and Treasure House books are available at Christian bookstores and distributors worldwide.

For a U.S. bookstore nearest you, call 1-800-722-6774.
For more information on foreign distributors, call 717-532-3040.
Reach us on the Internet: www.destinyimage.com.

ISBN 13 TP: 978-0-7684-0307-7
ISBN 13 Ebook: 978-0-7684-8779-4

For Worldwide Distribution, Printed in the U.S.A.

1 2 3 4 5 6 7 8 / 16 15 14 13 12

DEDICATION

I dedicate this book to my dad, Daniel. Thank you for teaching me financial wisdom over the years. Thank you for assisting me at times, and thank you for forcing me to walk by faith at other times. I have learned to say, "God, You've got mail!"

ACKNOWLEDGMENTS

First and foremost, I want to thank the Lord for His unfailing, unconditional love for me. Thank You, Lord, for saving my soul at a young age and filling me with Your precious Holy Spirit. It's a privilege and honor to write, speak, or record the Word of the Lord.

To my daughter, Destiny—thank you for filling my life with such joy. You always keep me laughing, even in the midst of challenges. I am so proud of you, and I know God is going to do great things through your life.

To my family and friends—thank you for believing in me, for encouraging me along the way, and for helping out during the writing process of this book.

To my spiritual mentors—thank you for being godly examples and leading the way for me to come into my full potential.

To the most awesome staff and intercessors that anyone could ever have, the Joy Ministries Team—thank you for standing with me through prayer, long hours of work, and your mountain-moving faith. Thank you for your passion for the Lord, your desire to see souls saved, and your heart to see lives changed. We truly are a team, and without you, Joy Ministries would not be what it is today.

To my most precious partners—without your giving of time, prayer, and financial support, Joy Ministries could not do everything it is doing today—thank you! Together we are transforming lives, healing hearts, and saving souls.

Finally, to my amazing editor and the entire team at Destiny Image—thank you for your heart to minister to people through printed material. Thank you for believing in me and for being such a great team to work with. I'm excited to partner together to change lives!

ENDORSEMENTS

When will the Body of Christ take on the Lord's yoke of peace and potential? This book allows the reader to see a new perspective of taking on the yoke of encouragement. In the chapter on having no reason for fear, Danette's book really resonated with me.

There is so much potential in the Church that seems to be in hiding, waiting to be discovered, re-discovered, revealed, or activated. What's holding them back? Fear! Fear clouds the fact that God created humankind to take dominion of the earth and not just populate it. This book unleashes the reasons to be activated now into your Kingdom destiny.

Danette explains in her book that she heard these words from the Lord, "If you are going to fulfill the call I have on your life, you must doubt your doubts and face your fears." Fear is a huge mountain for most when it comes to leaving their past failures behind and running toward their future.

It's time to overcome the fears that, according to Scripture, our Lord and Savior, Jesus, has already overcome. This book will encourage the reader to go and proclaim with confidence, "'The *kingdom of heaven is at hand.' Heal the sick, raise the dead, cleanse the lepers, cast out demons. Freely you have received, freely give"* (Matt. 10:7-8 NKJV).

Rev. H. Wade Trump III
Jamestown Christian Fellowship
Williamsburg, Virginia

Danette Crawford's book, *God, You've Got Mail,* is a must-read for all ages during these challenging economic times. I personally love the testimonies she shares about how, time and time again, she was required to pass the test of trusting God for her financial provision. I could relate to each humorous story, and I'm sure, as a reader, you will too!

D.J. Dozier
Former running back, Minnesota Vikings and Detroit Lions
Former outfielder, New York Mets and San Diego Padres

It is all about trust and the circumstances beyond our control that undermine our trust in God on a daily basis. Danette Joy Crawford has proven again that she has authority to speak to our heartstrings and heartaches in the battles she has fought and won. Her victory is ours as we read these compelling and compassionate accounts of our great God who knows what to do with our mail in His hands.

Dr. Joseph Umidi
Professor, Regent University, Divinity School
Senior Director, New Life Ministries International

Danette Crawford has hit another home run. In this, her latest book, the context is about forwarding all the bad news mail to God that we receive. God's answers to fifteen typical, even desperate appeals for good news in His return mail are abundantly supported by excerpts from His Word. To help Christians live true to these promises from God, a matching, faith-based "key" is provided to unlock each of them. This kind of mail you do not want to miss.

WILLIAM F. COX JR., PHD.
Professor and Founder
Christian Education Programs
School of Education, Regent University

Few people in life are willing to reveal their inner selves. Pastor Danette Crawford opens the door to her soul, revealing the darkest moments of her life, and walks us through her daily "mail call" with God. This book will be a blessing to the Body of Christ! Enlightening, emotional, and empowering!

PASTOR DAN WILLIS
Founder and Senior Pastor
The Lighthouse Church of All Nations
Alsip, Illinois

Contents

GOD, YOU'VE GOT MAIL!

It was a beautiful day in autumn. The leaves were beginning to change, and they displayed a stunning array of colors. However, the weather on the inside of our small home was quite different. It was the last day of the month, and tension was mounting as I faced the realization that my next mortgage payment was due the following day.

During this unexpected season in my life—the season of single motherhood—the financial pressures were great. Not only did I have the responsibilities of caring for an infant 24/7, but I was also shouldering the financial obligations of our household by myself. Alone. And that's how I felt—alone. But I would soon come to know my heavenly Father as my provider in a way I never would have imagined.

Our court date had been strategically delayed time and time again as my husband repeatedly avoided the scheduled hearings. It took several months to establish the amount he would pay me in child support, and even after that was done, his chronically delinquent payments had me returning to court at least two or three more times to have a court order enforced.

Every month after my separation from my husband, I worked hard at walking in total obedience to the Lord. It wasn't easy, but I did my best to fulfill what I felt the Lord was directing me to do. And a lot of the time, His instructions seemed very illogical. He once told me to "Get up out of your mess" and go do what I was called to do. I was willing to obey, but I wondered, *What about all of my financial concerns?* The child support payments were not enough to meet all of our needs, and we had to walk by faith in God's provision. As I sought to walk in obedience to my heavenly Father, I would repeatedly say, "Okay, God. I know it's Your will for me to pay my bills and to pay them on time."

I would continue in my conversation with the Lord, all the while thinking to myself, *If I can't pay my bills this month, I'm going to get a secular job.* I had earned a master's degree in counseling that I could have fallen back on, but I definitely didn't want to work as a counselor. I had enough problems of my own. I remember thinking, *I can see it now—someone will walk into my office with her "problem," and I'll want to slap her because what I'm going through will be so much worse than her little situation.*

So, I knew that job wouldn't work. I was really convinced that I needed a "no-brainer" job—a position that would allow me to work my scheduled hours and then go home, without any extra work or emotional baggage. I thought, *I know—I'll go work at Wal-Mart.* I wanted to be the person who stood at the door, handed out stickers, and said, "Thank you for shopping at Wal-Mart" all day long.

So every month, when it came time to pay my mortgage, I'd threaten God. It's funny now, looking back, but it sure wasn't funny at the time. I'd say, "Okay, God. If Your will is for me to keep doing what I'm called to do, then fine. But if I can't pay my mortgage this month, I'm going to work at Wal-Mart." I had this

conversation with the Lord at the end of every month. And at the end of every month, the Lord came through. It might have been at 11 o'clock the night before my payment was due, but He always put the money in my hand.

I began to treat every incoming bill as if it didn't have my name on it. When I would go to my post office box and find a pile of bills, I'd simply look up and say, "God, You've got mail!"

How could I say this, and with such confidence, you ask? Because I knew what God says to me—the promises He has put in His Word, which include abundant provision. When we know what God has promised to us, we can seize those promises and stand in faith until we receive them. This is the ultimate key to living in abundant provision.

Those who take the Lord at His word and believe He will fulfill what He has promised are automatically blessed because of their faith. A good example of someone who did just this was Mary, the mother of Jesus, when she was informed by an angel that she would be the mother of the Messiah. She immediately responded in faith, saying, *"I am the Lord's servant...May it be to me as you have said"* (Luke 1:38). Her words present a stark contrast with the reaction of Zechariah, Jesus' uncle, when he discovered that his wife, Elizabeth, would bear a son.

> *Zechariah asked the angel, "How can I be sure of this? I am an old man and my wife is well along in years." The angel answered, "I am Gabriel. I stand in the presence of God, and I have been sent to speak to you and to tell you this good news. And now you will be silent and not able to speak until the day this happens, because you did not believe my words, which will come true at their proper time"* (Luke 1:18-20).

Zechariah responded with words of unbelief. Consequently, he was prevented from speaking again until the angel's message had been fulfilled and his son, John the Baptist, was born.

Faith is just one key—an important one—to walking in God's abundant provision. Throughout this book, that's what we're going to learn—how to receive His inexhaustible supply for every one of our needs. The good news is, it doesn't depend on us, first and foremost. Our heavenly Father is ready to bless us above and beyond our expectations, if only we'll trust Him and believe in His promises. In *God, You've Got Mail,* we're going to discover all of the promises we can stand on when we follow His ways and walk in obedience.

LITTLE KEYS TO ABUNDANT PROVISION

After returning from a miracle crusade years ago, I was earnestly seeking God and praying that He would use me as a conduit of miracles. I wanted His miraculous power to be a regular part of my ministry. So I sought the Lord in prayer and petitioned to Him to show me some keys to flowing in His power.

After several days of this, the Lord spoke to me and said, "It's the little keys that give you access to the place that not many are qualified to go." He placed an image in my mind—one of the file cabinets in my office. I keep this file cabinet locked, as it contains sensitive documents—payroll records, confidential personnel files, tax documents, and so on. Not everyone is qualified to open that file cabinet. Only the person who has the little key that corresponds to the lock may open it. (And that's me.) God said, "That's how it is with the miraculous." I realized that it's the "little keys" that give us access to the power of God and the miraculous, and we need to qualify before we gain access to the little keys that unlock that power.

The Lord went on to tell me that He desires for every person to qualify for those "little keys," but that not everyone is willing to pay the price for them. What a revelation! I thought it was going to be a "big key" to flowing in the miraculous. I thought

the Lord would tell me to go on a forty-day fast or do something "big." Instead, He began to show me "little keys" that were no less important, like obedience, favor, and faith. So as we explore God's promises to us, we're going to learn how to claim them as ours—by "unlocking" them with what I call "little" keys to abundant provision. Get ready to unlock your miracle!

CHAPTER 1

"I AM MORE THAN ABLE TO MEET YOUR NEEDS"

And my God will meet all your needs according to his glorious riches in Christ Jesus.

—Philippians 4:19

I had to deal with financial hardship long before I became a single mother. During and after college, I traveled as an evangelist, and I relied completely on monetary contributions from other people. In this phase of my life, I would often look around and think, *Okay, who's going to help me now?* The truth was, I had already learned that God would provide for me. Whenever the funds I owed to a particular convention center or other venue didn't come in from the collection I took at the church where I was preaching, then the money would be waiting for me in my mailbox when I got home. Yet, even though I knew in my mind that I ought to trust God, it took awhile for my heart to catch up and internalize that lesson.

Learning to Trust the Lord as Provider

I was preparing for a city-wide youth crusade, and I was excited because I knew that a lot of young people would be saved and ministered to. But the question kept nagging me: Where in the world would I gather enough financial support? Many people had made a commitment to give money, but when it came down to it, they had backed out for various reasons. Just days before the payment was due, I was ministering at a Sunday morning service in a small church several hours away. As the service came to a close, I still didn't have enough funds to cover the payment, which was due the next day. I felt the Lord leading me to drive to Oklahoma City that afternoon to attend an evening service there. I wasn't even thinking about the possibility of collecting funds there, because I wasn't scheduled to minister in Oklahoma City. Yet I felt very strongly that the Lord was telling me to go there. So I got in the car with my young companion, Shea, and we drove to Oklahoma City. We arrived just in time for the evening service.

Much to my surprise, the youth pastor who was leading the service began to talk about our upcoming youth crusade! Someone in the congregation stopped him and said, "The young lady evangelist who's holding the event is here tonight." The youth pastor then asked me to come up to the platform and share about the crusade. I did, and when I had concluded my remarks, he took the microphone back from me and said to the congregation, "This is a God thing, and if God tells you to help her in any way, please do."

As the service let out, Shea and I moved about on our own, shaking hands with the congregants and talking to some of them. When the crowd had dispersed, I was left standing alone—without having received any financial gifts. I met up with Shea, and we

started making our way outside to our van. Shea said, "Did you see that lady in the last row who was in a wheelchair?"

"No," I replied.

"After the service, she motioned for me to come over to where she was, and she asked what we needed," Shea went on. "I told her, 'Seven thousand dollars by tomorrow morning,' and she wrote me a check!"

Talk about something to shout about! We were both excited and bewildered. But then, worry put a damper on my excitement as I thought, *What if her check isn't any good?*

The next morning, Shea and I went straight to the bank. When we presented the check to the teller and asked her to cash it, a strange expression crossed her face. She asked us to take a seat in the waiting area for a minute. My mind began to go wild with worry. *This is a bad check, and they think we're responsible*, I thought to myself. *What if they're calling the police? What if this? What if that?* The minutes that passed felt like an eternity. Finally the teller returned to the window. She apologized for the inconvenience and told us that she had called the woman whose name was on the account to verify that she'd written the check for $7,000. She then informed us that everything was fine, and she cashed the check. Hallelujah!

The Lord taught me a valuable faith lesson that day—to trust Him to provide, even if it meant relying on the least likely of avenues. The last person I would have expected the necessary funds to come from was a lady in the back row of a church in Oklahoma City where I hadn't even been scheduled to speak. Part two of that lesson was when God said, "You had enough faith to get that check into your hand, but you didn't have enough faith to believe that it was good." It's true—I didn't. But God was teaching me to look to Him alone, and never to people, for my provision.

You Never Know How He'll Meet Your Needs

Father God will always get His provision into our hands, but the channel through which He sends it is often the channel we would consider the least likely. I'm convinced that the Lord "sets us up" to build us up. The "setup" is that the funds never come from the expected source, and the "build-up" is for our faith. Father builds our faith on every step of this marvelous journey we are on with Him, as long as we trust Him.

Look to the Lord Alone

When we are in the midst of financial pressure, we have to be careful not to get angry and upset with those around us whom we think should be helping us. This is true for all of us, no matter our position—whether we're single parents, businesspeople, pastors, and so forth. We should always look to the Lord for our provision and not rely on the arm of the flesh.

God taught me this principle long before I became a single mom, but I forgot this particular faith lesson when met with the mounting financial pressures I faced when I was suddenly in the position of having to care for a newborn baby on my own and without a steady source of income. Basically, my faith in God's provision went out the window.

One day, as I stood staring at my file cabinet and pondered the bulging folder of bills marked "Due," I began to get angry. *My dad could write one check and pay off every one of my bills*, I thought, *and he wouldn't even miss the money.* As the bitterness mounted in my heart, the Lord spoke to me. "It's not his responsibility to pay your bills now that you are grown," He said. "But I'm your heavenly Father, and I can write one check and pay every bill you

have. And I definitely wouldn't miss it, because I own it all." He went on to say that He not only could, but He would, if I would only trust Him.

Wow! God has a way of getting right to the point with a word of truth. The truth was, I shouldn't have been looking to my dad—or any person, for that matter—to be the source of my provision. My heavenly Father was just waiting for me to look to Him. And today, your heavenly Father is waiting for you to look to Him for your every need. Jesus instructed us to pray, *"Give us this day our daily bread"* (Matt. 6:11 NKJV). It doesn't say, "Give us this day our monthly bread"; it says *"our daily bread."* I don't know about you, but I kind of like to have the whole month budgeted out. And if at all possible, I like to know my budget for the upcoming year! But God doesn't usually work that way. His way requires us to place our trust in Him and to walk by faith.

It's in His Hands

God got through to me loud and clear that day—so clear, in fact, that I began to treat every incoming bill as if it didn't have my name on it. As I mentioned before, I started leaving it up to God. When I would go to my post office box and find a pile of bills, I'd simply look up and say, "God, You've got mail!" Then I'd take God's mail home with me and place it in the folder labeled "Due." I wouldn't open that folder again until the money was put in my hand. At that time, I'd say, "Okay, God. Which of Your bills do You want me to pay for You?"

My mortgage payments, utility bills, and all other expenses were always paid on a monthly basis, despite my lack of a steady income. Even with my ex-husband's delinquent child support payments, God saw to it that we never paid a single bill late.

ALL THAT YOU HAVE COMES FROM HIM

The Lord taught me that everything I have comes from Him. Every dollar, every meal, every piece of clothing—everything I have comes from Him. He taught me to ask Him what He wanted me to do with every dollar that came into my hand—that was an important key to having all of my needs met. After all, we have this assurance in Philippians 4:19: *"My God shall supply all your need according to His riches in glory by Christ Jesus"* (NKJV). If my needs aren't met, something is wrong. Maybe I spent God's money on something I wanted or thought I needed instead of paying one of His bills. As we learn to ask God what He wants us to do with every dollar He puts into our hands, we can be free from stress and worry. When we receive bills in the mail, we can simply look to the Lord and say, "God, You've got mail!"

TRUST YOUR PROVIDER, NOT YOUR PROVISION

The Lord often tests us—a truth I was shocked to discover as a new Christian. In Exodus, we have an example of God testing the children of Israel for several reasons, but primarily to see whether they would respond in obedience and to gauge their heart attitude toward money. It was a setup to see whether they would trust in God and rely on Him to provide for their daily needs on a daily basis.

God provided food to the Israelites while they were fleeing Egypt. It came in the form of manna, which fell daily from heaven.

The LORD said to Moses, "I will rain down bread from heaven for you. The people are to go out each day and gather enough for that day. In this way I will test them and see whether they will follow my instructions" (Exodus 16:4).

A passing score on the Israelites' part would have been one that proved their complete faith and trust in the true Provider,

not their provision. And this is a test that each of us must pass. Sometimes we get so used to trusting in our provision—our paycheck, for example—that we lose sight of the One from whom it came. We just cruise through life, never realizing that our trust has shifted from the Source of everything to our salaries. When this happens, our trust in God weakens to the point where, if we lose a job, go through a divorce, or face an overwhelming situation that causes financial strain, we find it hard to hang on because the thing we've trusted in is slipping through our fingers.

Our heavenly Father promises to supply our daily bread—all of our needs (see Phil. 4:19). But we can't plead the promises of God if we aren't living by faith in God. One covenant benefit of being a child of God is the confidence that He will keep His part of the covenant and supply whatever we need. We need to rest in that!

TRUST IN HIS PROMISES

When you go to the doctor's office for a checkup, the receptionist asks you to produce your insurance benefits card. So what do you do? You pull it out of your wallet with confidence because you know you have benefits! You don't say, "I have benefits, but I'll go ahead and pay for this visit out of pocket." That would be foolish. And it's the same when it comes to our covenant benefits as children of the King. Pull out your list of benefits—the Bible—to find a detailed compilation of all of the covenant blessings that belong to you. Those blessings include health, provision, peace, and joy, to mention just a few!

Heaven doesn't have any bread shortages, so don't walk around with your head hanging low. Hold your head up and boldly stand on the Word—your benefit Book—as you trust God to give you your daily bread. Your means of provision may change, but your Provider is the same yesterday, today, and forever (see Heb. 13:8).

Psalm 37:25 says, *"I was young and now I am old, yet I have never seen the righteous forsaken or their children begging bread."* So don't worry. God has never forsaken the righteous, and He isn't about to abandon you. Never will you need to beg for bread. You may need to exercise your faith in Him to receive your daily bread, but that's a great place to be, because your intimacy with the Father grows as you rely on Him more and more.

Building Trust by "Just Enough"

When the children of Israel were crossing over from the land of "not enough" (Egypt) to the land of "more than enough" (the Promised Land), they had to walk through the land of "just enough" (the desert). In the desert, they had just enough for that day. They didn't lack, yet they didn't have an abundance of food or provisions. They had just enough—their daily bread, or manna, from heaven.

Similarly, when Jesus commissioned the twelve apostles, He gave them the following instructions: *"Take nothing for the journey except a staff—no bread, no bag, no money in your belts. Wear sandals but not an extra tunic"* (Mark 6:8-9).

Whenever we cross over to a new place or ascend to a higher level, we come through a period in which we have to rely on what I call the "daily bread." Why is this period necessary to pass through as we move up to the next level? Because the next level will require an increase in faith and trust in God.

Every time our ministry is about to cross over to the next level, I'm required to walk through the land of "just enough." It isn't fun, but what should we expect from a process that's meant to kill the flesh? This is the reason many people choose to remain in their comfort zones rather than crossing over into their "potential zones."

Over the years, each time our ministry has outgrown its office space and decided to relocate to a larger facility, the larger facility inevitably cost more—and I had to believe God to give us the extra funds every month. As I stepped out in faith, we had just enough to make each monthly payment. We never had any extra money, but we always had just enough to meet the payment. It was as if God was doling out our daily "manna" during these seasons of crossing over to the next level.

The same process applied to me as a homeowner. When I first bought my house, I had just enough money to pay the mortgage and utility costs every month. Groceries weren't even in my budget! But God always made sure that I had enough, even if it didn't look very promising on paper. It's during this "daily bread" stage that we are continually stretched and our faith is challenged to grow. These seasons are never comfortable to the flesh because they are designed to rid us of all waste and excess. The flesh has to be disciplined in order for us to climb to a higher level.

Don't Get Too Comfortable, or You Might Just Get Stuck

One problem with our flesh is that it likes the familiar. We grow comfortable with what we know, to the point where, when God calls us to journey to a better place, we don't feel like moving. The manna for the Israelites was a temporary provision. God didn't plan for them to remain in the desert dining on manna for the rest of their lives. It was their provision for the process of crossing over to the Promised Land—the land of more than enough. They could have made the transition in a matter of eleven days, but because of their grumbling, complaining, and unbelief, they took forty years to cross over. Imagine—four decades of eating manna!

When your manna begins to dry up, it doesn't mean you are going backward. It means you are going forward—forward into the Promised Land. Exodus 16:35 says, *"The Israelites ate manna forty years, until they came to a land that was settled; they ate manna until they reached the border of Canaan."* They were given manna until they crossed over to the destination God had been leading them to all along.

In my own life, as well as in the lives of others, I have seen the "manna" begin to dry up on the precipice of a divine destination. At that point, the flesh screams out, "Don't mess with my manna!" The provision I initially resented has become familiar, and my flesh resists any further growth that's required for me to cross over to a new place, even if it's a better place.

I was ministering in a city when I met a Christian woman in need of physical healing. In the middle of a miracle service, the Holy Spirit began to move in her, and she received her healing. Later, she told me that instead of rejoicing over the healing she had received, the first thing she thought was, *Oh, no! I'm not going to receive my disability check any longer.*

When God messes with our manna, we can get a little worried if we have been depending on the manna for any length of time. Due to the financial strains I faced after my husband left, I became a participant in the government-sponsored Women, Infants, and Children (WIC) program when my daughter, Destiny, was very young. I received formula, cereal, milk, peanut butter, and a couple of other items each month. We were beneficiaries of this program for about eighteen months, while I got back on my feet, financially. One day, when I was filling out the paperwork to reenroll in the program, the Lord spoke to me and said that it was time to get off the "manna." I reached the part where it asked me to write the income I expected for the next six months. As I went to fill in the amount, the Holy Spirit spoke to me again, saying, "Is that what you are expecting?" I had been praying for God to increase my monthly income to a certain amount—an amount that would have disqualified me from the WIC program. I was faced

with a dilemma: trust in God or trust in WIC—the "manna" I had grown accustomed to relying on. I knew I could count on my manna. What was I going to do without it?

I was going to cross over to the next level—that's what I was going to do! I wasn't going to need my manna any longer, but I needed to take a step of faith. I decided not to reenroll in the program, and I never went back on WIC in the years that followed because I knew God had spoken to me, even though my flesh was screaming out for the manna.

It was amazing! Very soon after I obeyed the Holy Spirit, my income increased—sure enough, by an amount that exceeded the WIC guidelines. What is the manna in your life that has begun to dry up? Don't get nervous when God messes with your manna—it's a good sign. It means that you are about to cross over to your Promised Land, the land of more than enough. Don't get stuck on the manna. God has something much better for you.

God Is All You Need

When you take what you have and you look to the Lord, you will always have more than enough. Remember, He owns everything; it's impossible to "overdraw" on your account of covenant blessings from Him!

A good illustration to help you remember this truth is found in the biblical account of the feeding of the five thousand. Matthew 14:19 says,

> ...Taking the five loaves and the two fish and looking up to heaven, he gave thanks and broke the loaves. Then he gave them to the disciples, and the disciples gave them to the people.

Jesus took what he had—that was His starting point. And that's where most people quit. They look at their resources, and they get depressed and discouraged, feel sorry for themselves, or try to manipulate others to give them resources. Just simply take what you have.

Second, Jesus looked up to heaven. Don't look down—look up and hold your head up. This is where your faith and your trust come in.

Then, third, Jesus gave thanks. Stop complaining about what you don't have and start praising God for what you do have. A grateful heart of thanksgiving is always a forerunner for an increase in blessing. If you aren't thankful for what you have, why would God give you more?

Fourth and finally, Jesus took a step of faith. Although He had only five loaves and two fish, He started giving out what He had—now that was a step of faith! When we take a step of faith and just start doing what we know we should do, provision will always be there.

Matthew 14:20-21 says,

They all ate and were satisfied, and the disciples picked up twelve basketfuls of broken pieces that were left over. The number of those who ate was about five thousand men, besides women and children.

They all ate—all five thousand men, along with an additional number of women and children! Not only did they all eat, but they were all satisfied. They didn't just get an appetizer. No one left hungry. And on top of that, there were twelve basketfuls left over! Don't tell me that God doesn't do big things with small resources. He rarely did big things with big resources, but He always did big things with small resources.

Father God wants you to take what you have, look to Him, give thanks, and then take a step of faith as you walk in obedience. Don't despise small beginnings. Don't let the size of your resources, the size of your storm, or the size of your perceived mistakes hold you back. Father owns it all, and He is ready and willing to meet all your needs!

LITTLE KEYS TO ABUNDANT PROVISION

Key #1: Trust your Provider, not your provision.

QUESTIONS FOR REFLECTION AND PERSONAL APPLICATION

1. Have you ever found yourself faced with a financial need that you never would have been able to meet on your own? What was the outcome?

2. Do you make a habit of seeking the Lord's will regarding how you manage your money? If so, what kind of direction has He given you in this area? If not, what can you do to invite God to become more involved in your fiscal management?

3. Have you ever passed up an opportunity for promotion or progress because you were "stuck" in the familiar? What was the result?

Prayer

Ask God to help you to trust Him as your provider and to rely on Him to meet your needs as you seek to obey His Word and follow His will.

Chapter 2

"It's Nothing for Me to Take Care of You"

Do not set your heart on what you will eat or drink; do not worry about it. For the pagan world runs after all such things, and your Father knows that you need them. But seek his kingdom, and these things will be given to you as well.

—Luke 12:29-31

In 1998, my husband moved out, and I was left with a tiny newborn and a great big God. I quickly learned that all I needed was a great big God! As long as I kept my eyes on the Lord, everything was fine. It was when I started to focus on myself and my situation that I would start to be overwhelmed with stress and feel sorry for myself. Whenever this happened, I would send out invitations for pity parties in the form of phone calls to anyone who would listen to me complain about how bad I had it. In the midst of my "invitation distribution," the Holy Spirit would whisper in my heart, "Get your eyes off of yourself. Keep your eyes on Me and your heart on the needs of My people." Even though I had considerable needs of my own, the Lord would remind me that there was always someone who was hurting worse than I was. There was always someone who was going through a situation worse than mine. The key to coming successfully through the devastation of divorce and the stress of becoming a single mom overnight was keeping my eyes off of myself.

Maybe you endured a similarly devastating shock overnight. Maybe you lost your job or had your home seized by the bank. May I encourage you today? There are many people who have never owned a home to lose. There are many people who have never held a paying job such as the job you lost. Please understand that I'm not trying to minimize your loss. I'm just trying to get you to bring things into perspective. When we get our eyes off of ourselves, it's much easier to see clearly. A focus on self blurs our vision and prevents us from seeing things the way God would have us see them. When we focus on ourselves, that's the only thing we see clearly! And one of the worst things is to be consumed with ourselves and our circumstances.

IT'S A FINE LINE BETWEEN NEEDS AND WANTS

Even those who have a lot of money tend to complain that they are hurting financially. The reason is that it's all relative—it depends on your salary, your savings, and your lifestyle. Most people would probably say that they're hurting financially, when it's actually their flesh that's hurting, not their finances. They may be disappointed because they can't afford a car that costs $200,000, while someone a few blocks over may not be able to afford a car that costs $2,000. The people who are really hurting financially are those who can't afford to feed their children. I'm not talking about the people who can't afford to take their family to a five-star restaurant every night. I'm talking about those who have no food in the pantry or the family who's living in their car because their house was repossessed.

In pursuit of the American dream, so many people get caught up in chasing the American idol—money! It's not wrong for us to have money and things, but it is wrong for money and things to "have" us!

When Jesus was teaching His disciples to pray, He instructed them to say, *"Give us each day our daily bread"* (Luke 11:3). I don't know about you, but I'd really rather not pray for daily bread, as I've said before. I'm a planner. I'm an administrator. I would prefer to pray for and receive my "monthly" bread up-front. If it were possible, I'd take my "yearly" bread, too, and ration it over the course of the next twelve months. But the Word says "daily." And the good news is, again, there's no "bread" shortage in heaven. As soon as we ask, the bread is released. There will always be enough when we appropriate it according to the will of our heavenly Father.

BLESSED FOR A REASON

The Lord wants to bless us in radical ways—to go above and beyond meeting our needs—but we often fail to understand why. The reason He bestows financial blessings upon us is for the fulfillment of kingdom purposes. Yes, Father God will meet all of our needs; yes, He will give us the desires of our hearts; but He will not settle for any position but first place in our lives. He wants to be our first love. Exodus 34:14 commands us, *"Do not worship any other god, for the LORD, whose name is Jealous, is a jealous God."* When the Lord is our first love, the foremost desire of our hearts is to see Daddy's kingdom built up. Our desire to reach the lost will be so strong that we don't mind how deep we need to dig into our pockets to do our part.

Blessed for Heeding, Not for Hoarding

The Gospels of Luke and Matthew record what we call the Lord's Prayer, which is what Jesus used to teach His disciples how to pray. After *"Give us today day our daily bread,"* it says, *"Forgive us our debts, as we also have forgiven our debtors. And lead us not into temptation, but deliver us from the evil one"* (Matt. 6:11-13). Immediately after praying for our daily bread, we are to pray that we will not fall into temptation. I have found that one of the areas in which we are tempted the most is in regard to our daily bread.

Sometimes, we are tempted to hoard up our "daily" bread for years to come. We create a sense of security—a false sense of security, I might add—when we have set aside a huge stash of "bread." When we amass reserves of stuff, it reveals a fearful spirit and a lack of trust in God. Instead of trusting the Lord with all of our hearts, as we are told to do in Proverbs 3:5, we rely on our own abilities and trust in the provisions we amass for ourselves. Don't get me wrong; I'm not saying that we shouldn't save money! Some people fail to plan for tomorrow because their flesh is caught up in the lusts of the moment. But it's wrong to hoard up today's manna for selfish reasons.

Jesus told a parable to illustrate this point:

Then [Jesus] said…, "Watch out! Be on your guard against all kinds of greed; a man's life does not consist in the abundance of his possessions." And he told them this parable: "The ground of a certain rich man produced a good crop. He thought to himself, 'What shall I do? I have no place to store my crops.' Then he said, 'This is what I'll do. I will tear down my barns and build bigger ones, and there I will store all my grain and my goods. And I'll say to myself, "You have plenty of good things laid up for many years. Take life easy; eat, drink and be merry."' But God said to him, 'You fool! This very night your life will be demanded from you. Then who will get what you have

prepared for yourself?' This is how it will be with anyone who stores up things for himself but is not rich toward God" (Luke 12:15-21).

One definition of *hoard* is "to accumulate money, food, or the like, in a hidden or carefully guarded place for preservation, future use, etc." Saving money, as an aspect of prudent fiscal management, is different from hoarding. One simple way to determine whether we are saving or hoarding is our response when God asks us to dip into our stash. The attitude with which we give to God and His kingdom is a good gauge of our heart condition and an indicator of whether we are saving or hoarding.

Let's say that you work for years to save up a nest egg, and then, one day, the Lord asks you to give a significant amount to your church or a ministry that's meeting the needs of His people. Would you obey cheerfully, or would you react like an old hen pecking at anyone who dared to come too close to her egg?

BLESSED TO TEST THE FLESH

Our flesh loves excess, and that's one of the reasons why we don't like to part with our "stash." We often receive a false sense of security from our savings account—a sense of security that is supposed to come from God alone.

Excess is defined as "an extreme or excessive amount or degree; superabundance." When it comes to our excess, we can save it, we can sow it, or we can blow it. Many times, our excess becomes waste, and God hates waste. The Word tells us that after Jesus fed the multitudes with the loaves and fishes, He instructed His disciples to gather up all of the leftovers (see John 6:5-13). He kept the scraps; He didn't throw them away. There is such wastefulness in our homes when it comes to food. When was the last time you ate leftovers? I'm guilty of bringing home the leftovers from dinner at a restaurant, only to throw them away a couple of days later.

That's wasteful! And I'm convinced that God hates waste, which is a common consequence of excess.

Our flesh loves excess because the flesh can never get enough. It's never satisfied, but always wants more—more food, a bigger house, a newer car. More, more, more!

When Moses was leading the Israelites out of their bondage in Egypt, they started grumbling and complaining about him—the very one who was the answer to their prayers. Moses was the one God had chosen to deliver His people from bondage. But as soon as the Israelites' flesh got uncomfortable, they started to gaze back longingly toward the place from which they had been delivered.

> *The Israelites said to* [Moses and his brother Aaron], *"If only we had died by the LORD's hand in Egypt! There we sat around pots of meat and ate all the food we wanted, but you have brought us out into this desert to starve this entire assembly to death"* (Exodus 16:3).

In Egypt, they had been in bondage, but their flesh had been comfortable on account of the excesses they'd enjoyed. The flesh always loves excess. When they left Egypt and arrived at a place where they needed to deal with their flesh—to set aside their carnal desires—they immediately started whining, wanting to return to their bondage. They would rather have been in bondage with excess than enjoying freedom with daily provision.

But excess quickly turns into waste, so it's crucial that we sow our excess into fruitful soil.

BLESSED WHEN WE "SOW IT" AND DON'T "BLOW IT"

Some of our most prized resources include our time, our energy, and our finances. When God blesses us with an excess of

resources, we are supposed to sow them into the work of the kingdom. Our excess is not for ourselves, but for others.

When you have an excess of time, invest it into the lives of others. Don't blow your time by sitting in front of the television watching programs that don't bring honor to God. Sow your time in prayer for others, or find someone who's lonely or needs encouragement.

When you have an excess of income, don't spend it all or move the entirety into your savings account. Invest into the kingdom of God. The Lord has given you excess for the benefit of others, not for selfish spending. The apostle Paul said the same thing in Second Corinthians 9:11: *"You will be made rich in every way so that you can be generous on every occasion, and through us your generosity will result in thanksgiving to God."* This verse tells us that God blesses us financially *"so that"* we can be a blessing to others.

Sometimes, we misinterpret the "so that." We think that God blesses us with extra finances "so that" we can go spend it on more clothes, more shoes, expensive vacations, and the like. When you think about it, you can really wear only so many pairs of shoes, and some of your best vacations were probably those you spent at home having quality time with your family. If we blow our excess income on ourselves, we have wasted it. When we sow it, we invest it. Remember, sow it; don't blow it!

Blessed as We Avoid the Snare of Money

He who dwells in the shelter of the Most High will rest in the shadow of the Almighty. I will say of the LORD, "He is my refuge and my fortress, my God, in whom I trust." Surely he will save you from the fowler's snare and from the deadly pestilence (Psalm 91:1-3).

43

When we dwell in the secret place of the Most High and when we're saying of the Lord what is true, we can count on Him to deliver us from the snare of the fowler. He will deliver us—but we first need to decide that we need deliverance!

The "*fowler's snare*" shows up in different forms for different people. In many cases, money is a snare, whether it traps the heart in greed or causes people such fear that it snags their faith and causes it to unravel.

Psalm 91:9-11 says,

If you make the Most High your dwelling—even the LORD, who is my refuge—then no harm will befall you, no disaster will come near your tent. For he will command his angels concerning you to guard you in all your ways.

The key word in this passage is *if*. *If* we make the Most High our dwelling, everything else will fall into place. Father God wants us to take up residence in His presence. When we do that, we can be confident that the blessings laid out in Psalm 91 are ours. The Lord will send angelic escorts to "*guard* [us] *in all* [our] *ways*," including our finances!

BLESSED AS WE PRACTICE PRUDENT FISCAL MANAGEMENT

The Book of Proverbs is filled with wisdom, and you will be amazed at how much of that wisdom has to do with fiscal management. I want to challenge you to read and meditate on Proverbs on a regular basis, if not on a daily basis. Here is just a sampling of wisdom from this book:

The sluggard craves and gets nothing, but the desires of the diligent are fully satisfied (Proverbs 13:4).

44

Lazy hands make a man poor, but diligent hands bring wealth (Proverbs 10:4).

Get-rich-quick schemes never work, and Proverbs even tells us so. Proverbs 28:19 says, *"He who works his land will have abundant food, but the one who chases fantasies will have his fill of poverty."* Not only do they not work, but you can become poor trying! But hard work—yes, I said hard work—brings an abundance. Proverbs 12:11 says, *"He who works his land will have abundant food, but he who chases fantasies lacks judgment."* It's not even wise, it's not even good judgment, to chase fantasies or get-rich-quick schemes. It's wise to work hard. After all, the first thing God ever gave to Adam in the Garden of Eden was a job!

Proverbs 14:23 says, *"All hard work brings a profit, but mere talk leads only to poverty."* All hard work is profitable! Even if you don't see the benefit or prosperity of your hard work right away, it's a biblical principle that *all* hard work is profitable.

I grew up on a farm, and my dad raised my siblings and me to be hard workers. Yet the current generation of young people seem to lack the work ethic I was taught. This seems to be the generation of video games and couch potatoes. Unfortunately, many young people don't know how to work hard at physical labor. For those of you called to the ministry, you'd better know how to work—hard. If you are afraid of physical labor and hard work, you'd better get another job! The desires of the diligent are not just satisfied—they are fully satisfied. It's diligent, hardworking hands, coupled with a heart of obedience, that prosper.

When it comes to accumulating wealth, saving takes a lot of self-discipline, especially when you are living on a shoestring budget to start with. To save money, you must establish a budget and then stick to it. Budgeting is the key to getting out of debt and staying that way, but a budget isn't any good if you aren't disciplined enough to stick to it.

The word *budget* has an effect on people that's similar to the word *diet*. At the mere mention of the word, most people cringe. But a diet does not necessarily prohibit you from eating any of the foods you enjoy. All it means is that you decide to show self-restraint in what you eat, with a focus on moderation. You master your flesh by denying it the luxury of "fleshing out" and indulging in whatever it wants, whenever it wants it.

A budget works the same way. It doesn't mean that you can't purchase anything for the purpose of enjoyment, just that you need to bring your flesh under the control of your spirit and be able to discern when to spend your money and when to forgo a certain purchase or expense.

You have to stop looking at the word *budget* as a bad word. A budget can be liberating and life-giving when you stick to it, because it releases you from bondage to debt.

The discipline that's required to budget effectively can be seen in the following illustration of the ant:

> *Go to the ant, you sluggard; consider its ways and be wise! It has no commander, no overseer or ruler, yet it stores its provisions in summer and gathers its food at harvest. How long will you lie there, you sluggard? When will you get up from your sleep? A little sleep, a little slumber, a little folding of the hands to rest—and poverty will come on you like a bandit and scarcity like an armed man* (Proverbs 6:6-11).

The ant is wise. Instinctively, it plans its provision for the next season by storing up enough for the days ahead. This process requires self-discipline and discernment, but if the ants can do it, so can we!

A lack of discipline can prove deadly (see Prov. 5:23). When you lack discipline, you can die—financially, emotionally, spiritually, and even physically. If you lack discipline to stop smoking,

you can die. If you lack discipline to stop eating, drinking, or doing drugs, you can die. Discipline is an important part of life that affects us in multiple areas. Budgeting is a form of discipline that may hurt the flesh for a season, but it always brings great rewards in return.

Lastly, taking on debt is a quick way of reaping a harvest you haven't earned. And it's a dangerous method. The Word tells us to *"owe no one anything except to love one another..."* (Rom. 13:8 NKJV). I'm not sharing this Scripture in a spirit of condemnation, but as an offering of wisdom. There is a young woman on my staff who first joined our team as an intern. She had a strong work ethic and a high standard of excellence in all of her work, not to mention a distinct call and anointing on her life, so I offered her a position and hired her as soon as her internship was completed.

When she joined our team, she started participating in all of our staff meetings, which include prayer meetings. One day, I heard a word from the Lord for her, and I shared it with her: God wanted her to attend graduate school without any debt, and He wanted her to trust Him to pay her bills. I then told her my own testimony of how God had supernaturally paid all of my bills in graduate school—as a result of my faith in His provision.

Don't go the "easy route" and take out a loan. Stand in faith on the promises of God, and He will give you what you need. Remember, where the Lord guides, He provides.

It Goes Deeper than Your Wallet

I was recently preparing to preach at one of our Breakthrough Miracle services, and the Lord spoke to me and said, "People coming tonight only think they need a breakthrough in their finances." He went on to show me that they really needed a breakthrough in their minds, in their faith, and in their flesh.

During the service, when I asked for a show of hands from those who needed a breakthrough in their finances, just about every person in the sanctuary raised a hand. I went on to share Scriptures to prove that their finances weren't the real problem, according to the Lord. I helped them to understand that some of them needed a breakthrough in their minds because they were filled with fear—the fear of having their needs go unmet. Others needed a breakthrough in their faith because they really didn't believe that God could and would supply their needs. And others needed a breakthrough in their flesh because their financial problems were rooted in excessive spending driven by fleshly desires for more, more, more.

We had an incredible service that night as the Holy Spirit put His finger on the root of the real problem in each person's life. The Word says that the truth you know will set you free (see John 8:32). That night, those people were set free when they learned the truth about their situations. It isn't enough to treat the symptoms—we must get right to the root of the problem. Sometimes, the Lord allows us to have an experience that gives us a faith adjustment or realignment in what—or who—we trust in. Other times, the Lord allows circumstances to come into our lives to reveal the fears that plague our minds or the fleshly desires that have gotten out of hand. Because of His love for us, the Holy Spirit gently leads us along the path of truth, granting us the breakthrough we really need.

LITTLE KEYS TO ABUNDANT PROVISION

Key #2: Sow it; don't blow it!

48

Questions for Reflection and Personal Application

1. Many people can identify with this observation: "The flesh loves excess." For some, the area in which they are prone to excess is not money, but clothing, technological gadgets, travel, or something else. Is there an area in which you struggle with tempering your excess? How have you sought to counteract this tendency?

2. When was the last time you blessed someone else with your "excess," whether it was money, time, physical labor, or something else? How did you feel afterward? Is this something you might consider committing to do on a regular basis?

3. A budget is a wise tool to manage your finances, and it isn't a bad thing; like a diet, a budget is "bad" only if you overindulge (in spending) and have to suffer the consequences. Have you established a budget to manage your finances? If not, consider setting one up. Start by spending one month recording where your money goes—categories such as groceries, utility bills, car payment/gasoline purchases, and so forth. Simply knowing your spending habits will help you to set limits in each category to better manage your money.

Prayer

Confess and repent of any wasteful habits and excessive spending you may have done. Then ask the Lord to fortify your self-discipline as you seek to practice frugality and to sow into His kingdom.

Chapter 3

"You Have No Reason to Fear"

Do not fear, little flock, for it is your Father's good
pleasure to give you the kingdom.

—Luke 12:32 NKJV

The topic of finances awakens a spirit of fear in so many people, including Christians. For some, financial fear started way back in childhood, when their families were experiencing financial hardship. Children are influenced significantly by the attitudes of their parents, especially if those attitudes embody fear, panic, and uncertainty. A sense of security—the confidence that all of their needs will be met—is extremely important for children. And everyone needs to feel loved, significant, and secure. Children who grow up without the confidence that their basic needs will be provided usually develop a sense of insecurity that can have dire consequences in their emotional and spiritual lives.

Those whose sense of security has been compromised, especially if it started in childhood, are often left vulnerable to the spirit of fear. Depending on the nature of the security of which they were robbed, people can experience fear in the areas of finances, health, emotions, and so forth. A child who was traumatized by sexual or physical abuse develops a sense of physical insecurity, and understandably so. And, without Christian counseling and the power of the Holy Spirit, that child may fall prey to fear so much that it dominates his or her life.

DOUBT YOUR DOUBTS AND FACE YOUR FEARS

The Lord spoke to me one day and showed me that I was filled with all kinds of fears—fears that were deeply rooted in my childhood. He said, "If you are going to fulfill the call I have on your life, you must doubt your doubts and face your fears." I was filled with so much doubt—doubt that I could continue to minister as a divorced single mom with a newborn daughter, doubt that we could make it financially. And those were just a few of my doubts.

The Lord then reminded me that the devil is a liar and the father of lies (see John 8:44) and, therefore, that everything he had been telling me was the opposite of the truth. The Lord said again, "You need to doubt those doubts." So whenever a doubt would come into my mind, I would simply say out loud, "I doubt that! I know God is going to provide. I doubt that—I know God is going to fulfill His call on my life." It worked. Faith began to grow in my heart, and the doubts slowly faded. It's true that *the tongue has the power of life and death…*" (Prov. 18:21). With our words, we speak life or speak death to our faith, our emotions, and our outcomes. Start speaking the Word of God over yourself and all that pertains to you, and faith will arise within your spirit.

After I learned to doubt my doubts, I had to face my fears. The first of my fears the Lord dealt with was the fear that I would not have my needs met. As a single parent, my mother struggled to provide for my brothers and me, and I was always acutely aware of the financial pressures she felt on a daily basis. She would discuss

her issues openly in front of us kids, never veiling her stress and anxiety. As a result, I grew up with a lot of worries over money.

Children should not be subject to the pressures of adulthood. They must be taught, first and foremost, that their heavenly Father will provide for them. When I was growing up, my mother didn't have a relationship with the Lord and neither did we kids. None of us knew that we had a heavenly Father who was ready to meet all of our needs—and then some. And so our family, like so many others, lived in a constant state of financial strain with no assurance of being provided for.

Then, years later, when I was a single mom myself, I was sitting on my bed, looking out the window at the beautiful clouds overhead, and I began to pray about our financial needs. Immediately, the Lord responded and said, "It's nothing for Me to take care of your little girl, your little house, and your little self." Wow! Father had spoken! And He had lovingly reassured me that He would provide for us. He was putting things into perspective for me. It was nothing for my great big God—the God of the universe—to provide for us. We were just a speck in this world, and it was nothing for God to provide for our speck-sized needs. The needs that seemed so big and overwhelming to me were really small to God. He was basically saying, "Consider it done!"

Pursue Peace

The years that followed were exciting to me, as I witnessed firsthand my Father's miraculous provision and began to conquer my fear of not having my needs met. Of course, the adventure was exciting instead of overwhelming only because of my daily decision to walk in faith. We have the choice, you know! Choose peace.

Jesus says,

Peace I leave with you; My [own] peace I now give and bequeath to you. Not as the world gives do I give to you. Do not let your hearts be troubled, neither let them be afraid. [Stop allowing yourselves to be agitated and disturbed; and do not permit yourselves to be fearful and intimidated and cowardly and unsettled] (John 14:27 AMP).

How about you? Are you allowing your heart to fill with worry and fear, or are you enjoying Father's promised peace and provision?

DEFEAT FEAR AND DISCOURAGEMENT

We have this assurance from God:

So do not fear, for I am with you; do not be dismayed, for I am your God. I will strengthen you and help you; I will uphold you with my righteous right hand (Isaiah 41:10).

We have no need to fear in our finances or in any other area. Never forget that fear and discouragement are some of Satan's favorite schemes to use against us. *"For God has not given us a spirit of fear, but of power and of love and of a sound mind"* (2 Tim. 1:7 NKJV). If God is never the source of fear, then you know that the enemy is the one who has brought it upon you. He tries to cripple you with fear—fear of rejection, fear of failure, fear of other people, and so forth. Yet God has given you all power and authority in the name of Jesus! (See Luke 9:1.) Don't throw away your power by receiving a spirit of fear from the pit of hell! Father God has given you the power to overcome anything that comes against you in this life. Jesus told His followers, and He tells us today, *"I have given you authority to trample on snakes and scorpions and to overcome all the power of the enemy; nothing will harm you"* (Luke 10:19). You are the one with the power! Never throw away your power from God, especially in exchange for a spirit of fear.

Not only do you have power, but you have love and a sound mind. The enemy likes to mess with your God-given need to give

and receive love. If you feel rejected, whether that rejection is real or perceived, you will shy away from showing love, as well as from receiving it. Yet we have been created to love and be loved because we were designed in the image of God, and *"God is love"* (1 John 4:8,16). When we are bound up in fear, the enemy isolates us behind a wall of rejection, and our need for love goes unmet. It's like a car without gas or any other energy source—it's not very productive.

Not only has God given us power and love, but He has made the provision for each of us to have a sound mind. Of course, the devil would prefer that the sound of his lies be what echoes in your mind on a daily basis: "Nobody loves you," "You are all alone," "You're different," "You don't have any friends," and so on. But your heavenly Father has given you a sound mind—a mind that is filled with the truth about you and your situation. Fill your mind daily with God's Word, and it won't leave any room for the devil's lies.

A sound mind is not plagued with thoughts of fear; it meditates on things above, not on things below (see Col. 3:2). In other words, it meditates on truth, not on the enemy's deceptions. Don't be deceived into thinking that your storm is out of God's control. It might be out of your control, but nothing is too hard for God to handle.

Philippians 4:8 shows us a key to living with a sound mind. It says,

> *Finally, brothers, whatever is true, whatever is noble, whatever is right, whatever is pure, whatever is lovely, whatever is admirable—if anything is excellent or praiseworthy—think about such things.*

Our greatest battles always begin in our minds. As we renew our minds daily to the truth of God's Word, we can maintain a sound mind in the midst of every challenge life throws our way—including financial challenges!

Joshua 1:8 says,

Do not let this Book of the Law depart from your mouth; meditate on it day and night, so that you may be careful to do everything written in it. Then you will be prosperous and successful.

Father God has given us the instructions, and now it's up to us to carry them out. He has clearly told us how to be prosperous and successful—by meditating on His Word, which is how we preserve a sound mind. We are not to *let* His Word depart from our mouths, meaning that it's up to us. If we get lazy and let the enemy fill our minds with his garbage, we have made a poor choice. No one can choose for you. You must choose to speak the Word daily and to meditate on it so that your tongue will bring life, not death. Remember the power Father said He gave you? A lot of that power is right under your nose—on your tongue! So speak the Word over yourself and your circumstances. Deny what the devil says, and affirm what the Lord has spoken.

Not only are we supposed to speak the Word daily, but we are also to do the Word daily. We're told to meditate on it day and night. In other words, we are to think about the truth—God's Word. Fill your mind with what the Bible says, *"so that you may be careful to do everything written in it."* In other words, do the Word!

So we speak the Word, think the Word, and do the Word. When you make a habit of these three practices, fear and discouragement will depart from you. James 4:7 says, *"...Resist the devil, and he will flee from you."* What better resistance than speaking, thinking, and doing the Word?

Our greatest battles always begin in our minds. After I was saved, the Lord started unpacking my emotional baggage. He began showing me how my damaged emotions were closely

connected to my mind—specifically, the thoughts I allowed the enemy to plague me with for so many years. As we renew our minds daily by the truth of God's Word, we can maintain a sound mind in the midst of every challenge life throws our way—even our financial challenges.

DEFEAT DEPRESSION

Depression and fear are closely connected. When fear is permitted to hang around for a while, it can easily turn into depression. You may have never recognized that fear is the root of your problem. Fear is the root of many things, and, when it goes undetected, depression can set in. Ask the Holy Spirit to show you if an underlying spirit of fear has caused you to get into a deep pit of despair. If so, you dig your way out of the pit by speaking, thinking, and doing the Word of truth.

No matter what your financial situation looks like in the natural realm, remember, God operates in the supernatural realm, and He owns it all.

Yours, O LORD, is the greatness and the power and the glory and the majesty and the splendor, for everything in heaven and earth is yours... (1 Chronicles 29:11).

The earth is the Lord's, and everything in it, the world, and all who live in it (Psalm 24:1).

God owns everything, so there's no need to fall into depression over the state of your bank accounts.

DISCOVER THE POWER OF PERFECT LOVE

The Father heart of God is filled with love for us—perfect love. *"There is no fear in love. But perfect love drives out fear, because fear has to do with punishment. The one who fears is not made perfect in love"* (1 John 4:18). God loves us unconditionally—today, tomorrow, and forever (see Heb. 13:8). And His love does not depend on the state of our bank accounts or the size of our wallets. Don't confuse the love of your heavenly Father with human love, which is fickle and, despite our best intentions, conditional, at least to a degree.

People are inconsistent. They may say that they love you one day, with actions to back it up, and then the next day, they may express something entirely different, depending on their mood. But God isn't like that.

> *God is not a man, that he should lie, nor a son of man, that he should change his mind. Does he speak and then not act? Does he promise and not fulfill?* (Numbers 23:19)

> *He who is the Glory of Israel* [God] *does not lie or change his mind; for he is not a man, that he should change his mind* (1 Samuel 15:29).

> *But from everlasting to everlasting the LORD's love is with those who fear him, and his righteousness with their children's children—with those who keep his covenant and remember to obey his precepts* (Psalm 103:17-18).

> *Every good and perfect gift is from above, coming down from the Father of the heavenly lights, who does not change like shifting shadows* (James 1:17).

Perfect love drives out fear, but imperfect, unhealthy love creates fear. Dysfunctional love and broken covenant relationships produce fear. Codependent and emotionally dependent relationships encourage and enhance fear. But perfect love drives out fear. Remember what the Lord said in Isaiah 41:9-10: *"...You are my servant, I have chosen you and have not rejected you. So do not fear, for I am with you...."* Because Father has chosen us and has not

58

rejected us, we don't have to fear—not even in the midst of great financial storms.

We need to allow the Holy Spirit to reveal and uproot any fear from our lives so that we may operate in God's provision for us—His power, His love, and the sound mind that comes from Him. We have been given Holy Spirit power to overcome anything we are faced with in life. Father wants us to be free to love and be loved. We can't love others in a healthy, godly way if we don't love ourselves. We can love ourselves in a healthy way only by knowing Christ's unconditional love for us. And praise God, Father has made provision for us to have a sound mind—a mind that is worry-free, filled with peace, and renewed to the truth of God's Word. A sound mind is not plagued with thoughts of fear and rejection, but it meditates on things above and not on things below (see Col. 3:2). In other words, it meditates on truth, not on the enemy's deceptions.

STAND FEARLESSLY IN YOUR WORK FOR THE LORD

First Corinthians 15:58 says,

Therefore, my dear brothers, stand firm. Let nothing move you. Always give yourselves fully to the work of the Lord, because you know that your labor in the Lord is not in vain.

When we are doing the work of the Lord, we can't allow anyone or anything to pull us away into detours and distractions. I want to encourage you to stand firm and let nothing move you, including your financial situation. I want to encourage you to stay where God has placed you. Don't dare move until you know without a shadow of a doubt that it's God who's moving you. The only thing that should move you is God Himself. The labor you are doing for His kingdom is not in vain, so stand firm. You should never make a decision according to your bank accounts, especially if that decision is motivated by fear. You should always make your decisions according to the leading of the Holy Spirit. God will often lead you to do things that seem as though you can't afford to do it because He is just waiting for your continual, faithful obedience. He's just waiting for you to stand and keep standing, and then that provision will be released. If the children of Israel would not have stepped into the water of the Red Sea, it never would have parted!

Nehemiah 2:10 says, *"When Sanballat the Horonite and Tobiah the Ammonite official heard about this, they were very much disturbed that someone had come to promote the welfare of the Israelites."* Nehemiah was doing the work of the Lord. He was helping the people rebuild their lives. And the enemy didn't like it one bit! Whether you are a pastor in the ministry, a professional in the "secular" realm trying to be a witness for Christ in your office, or a parent trying to raise godly children, the enemy sees your efforts for the kingdom of God. Do you think he likes that? Of course not! Don't fall for the tricks of the enemy. Don't allow him to distract or discourage you. Stand and keep on standing—the kingdom of God is counting on you!

STAND IN PRAYER

We need to stand in prayer as we wage spiritual warfare against the enemy. We need to stand in prayer against false accusations. When Nehemiah's enemies tried to hinder his work, he refused to talk to them. Nehemiah consulted with God alone about what the enemy was up to. Nehemiah didn't get on the level of the enemy. He didn't call all of his friends to talk about it. And he didn't quake in fear. He talked only to God!

The enemy tried to convince Nehemiah that his work was in vain, but that was nothing more than a big lie. The enemy was

attempting to discourage Nehemiah so that he would give up. But the proof was in the pudding—the wall was built in fifty-two days. So Nehemiah's work wasn't in vain, after all!

Nehemiah 4:20 says, *"Wherever you hear the sound of the trumpet, join us there. Our God will fight for us!"* Nehemiah stood in prayer. He kept working, but he prayed at the same time. He knew his God would fight for him, but he did his part—he prayed!

To stand effectively against the devil's schemes, we must have on our full armor. Ephesians 6:11 says, *"Put on the full armor of God so that you can take your stand against the devil's schemes."* Don't be naive about the enemy's schemes. Learn to identify them by the power of the Holy Spirit and stand against them. Intimidation, fear, discouragement—they are all schemes of the enemy to stop you from doing God's will for your life.

ASSUME YOUR POSITION

Your "position" should always be the position of God, which you get from His Word—the Holy Bible—as well as personal words from the Lord. If you haven't gotten a word from God regarding a particular situation, you should fast and pray until He speaks to you. And then, when you get a word, stand on it, and don't quit standing.

Second Chronicles 20:17 says,

You will not have to fight this battle. Take up your positions; stand firm and see the deliverance the LORD will give you, O Judah and Jerusalem. So not be afraid; do not be discouraged. Go out to face them tomorrow and the LORD will be with you.

You will see the deliverance the Lord is about to give you. Don't be afraid! Don't allow fear to attack you. You attack that spirit of fear with your faith, with God's Word, and with the word

God gives to you. Go face-to-face with the enemy. Don't run in fear. Don't shrink back. God is going to fight your battle, and very soon, you will be experiencing the victory, so hold your head up high and shout now!

FREE FROM FEAR

For you to penetrate to the next level in God, you must be free from the spirit of fear. Disappointments and times of discouragement can serve as an open door for fear. Rejection, abuse, and negative words can also serve as an open door for fear. No matter what door was opened, that spirit of fear must leave you, in the name of Jesus. The root of fear serves as a breeding ground for depression. But when the spirit of fear is uprooted, depression *must* go.

I believe that Father is ready to turn things around for you today. Say out loud, "It's turnaround time. Fear will no longer steal my power. Fear will no longer steal my love. And fear will no longer steal my sound mind!" Be encouraged—the best is yet to come.

LITTLE KEYS TO ABUNDANT PROVISION

Key #3: Doubt your doubts and face your fears.

QUESTIONS FOR REFLECTION AND PERSONAL APPLICATION

1. Do you experience fear in the area of your finances? If so, identify the lies the enemy has been whispering to you—"You'll never be able to pay your bills," "You'll always be in debt," "You can't afford that"—and

choose a promise from Scripture to contradict them. For example, if the enemy is telling you, "You'll never be able to pay your bills," tell him, *"My God will meet all my needs, according to His glorious riches in Christ Jesus"* (see Phil. 4:19).

2. Do you find that the degree to which you trust in God depends on the severity of your situation? Remember, He never changes (see Heb. 13:8). When faced with trials in any realm, go to God's Word and remind yourself that He will bring you through by reading Scriptures that relate to His power, strength, and wisdom.

Prayer

Confide in the Lord any particular fears you are facing, financial or otherwise. Then proclaim your belief that He will go above and beyond your expectations to meet your needs and conquer those fears. Finally, thank Him for His unfailing faithfulness and for granting you His peace that passes understanding.

CHAPTER 4

"I WILL GIVE YOU PEACE IN EVERY SEASON"

Peace I leave with you; my peace I give you. I do not give to you as the world gives. Do not let your hearts be troubled and do not be afraid.

—John 14:27

Within mere months, I went from living on two incomes to living on no income at all. Everything in life is subject to change, and change often happens overnight. The financial seasons of life change perhaps more than any other seasons because they depend so much on factors we can't control, such as the economy. The housing market is in constant flux; stocks on Wall Street are all over the place on any given day.

Maybe you are in a financial season of abundance today. Don't get too comfortable—it could change overnight! Or perhaps you are experiencing a season of drought and lack. This, too, shall pass! No matter the type of season we're in, we have this assurance in

Philippians 4:19: *"My God will meet all your needs according to his glorious riches in Christ Jesus."*

Regardless of the pattern of financial seasons in our earthly lives, what really counts is the season of eternity. Some people spend all of their lives preparing financially for retirement, yet they have not prepared financially for eternity.

> *Do not store up for yourselves treasures on earth, where moth and rust destroy, and where thieves break in and steal. But store up for yourselves treasures in heaven, where moth and rust do not destroy, and where thieves do not break in and steal. For where your treasure is, there your heart will be also* (Matthew 6:19-21).

All seasons, except for eternity, are temporary. We should be content and enjoy the season we are in, but we should always prepare for the season we know is coming—the season of eternity.

In the meantime, if we are in a season of abundance, it doesn't mean that we should be liberal in our spending; that would not be wise. The key is to balance our spending, our saving, and our sowing—our faithful giving to the kingdom of God through tithes and offerings. It's the financial seed sown into good ground for the work of the Lord that really counts, because it builds the only kingdom that endures forever. When we become members of that kingdom by accepting Jesus Christ as our Lord and Savior, we know where we're ultimately headed, and we can have true, lasting peace.

PURSUING THE PEACE THAT TRANSCENDS ALL CIRCUMSTANCES

Father God wants to give us His peace in every area of our lives. That sounds great, but it's actually a struggle for most people to receive His peace, especially in the area of their finances.

Again, Jesus said,

Peace I leave with you; My [own] peace I now give and bequeath to you. Not as the world gives do I give to you. Do not let your hearts be troubled, neither let them be afraid. [Stop allowing yourselves to be agitated and disturbed; and do not permit yourselves to be fearful and intimidated and cowardly and unsettled] (John 14:27 AMP).

Notice that He put the responsibility for our state of mind on our shoulders: *"Stop allowing yourselves to be agitated and disturbed; and do not permit yourselves to be fearful...."* Again, that's a lot easier said than done. But the only way to stop feeling agitated is to shift our focus away from the source of our agitation onto something that brings the opposite feeling. It isn't enough to look at our bank account and say, "I'm not bothered by this." We need to look to the Father and acknowledge that He is in control. Then and only then can we experience a sense of peaceful confidence that our needs will be met, regardless of how much money we have in the bank.

Maybe you are in the midst of a financial storm. Stop quaking and start calming the storm, just as Jesus did (literally speaking):

One day Jesus said to his disciples, "Let's go over to the other side of the lake." So they got into a boat and set out. As they sailed, he fell asleep. A squall came down on the lake, so that the boat was being swamped, and they were in great danger. The disciples went and woke him, saying, "Master, Master, we're going to drown!" He got up and rebuked the wind and the raging waters; the storm subsided, and all was calm. "Where is your faith?" he asked his disciples. In fear and amazement they asked one another, "Who is this? He commands even the winds and the water, and they obey him" (Luke 8:22-25).

Jesus is in your boat, so calm down! You can speak to your financial storm and force it to settle down. With Jesus in your boat, you don't need to worry about anything, and you can walk in peace. The key is to focus on Jesus and His promises. Where is your faith today? Is it sinking fast in a financial storm, or is it riding high above the waves?

DWELL IN THE SECRET PLACE

Peace and fear cannot coexist in our hearts or in our minds. If we allow the spirit of fear to come into any area of our lives, we will not have peace in that area until we dispel that fearful spirit. We must actively pursue peace as a powerful defense system against fear. And one way to do this is to dwell in the secret place of the Most High.

"He who dwells in the secret place of the Most High shall remain stable and fixed under the shadow of the Almighty [Whose power no foe can withstand]" (Ps. 91:1 AMP). Stop and think about it: What have you been dwelling on? Where has your mind been "hanging out"? When we dwell, or reside, in the presence of the Lord, we receive a constant supply of His peace, which enables us to defeat every fearful thought that comes to mind. Another result of dwelling in the presence of God is remaining stable. *Stable* is defined as "firmly established; enduring or permanent," as well as "steadfast; not wavering or changeable, as in character or purpose." Some people are stable one day, but become quickly unglued the very next day—in the same situation. Why does this happen? Because they started dwelling on the natural facts and stopped dwelling in the presence of their supernatural God.

When we put more stock in the opinions of people—the predictions of the newscasters, the positions of naysayers—we move out from the secret place of God and away from His all-surpassing peace. Never forget that the "facts" are no match for the truth—God's Word! What God says, goes, no matter the natural evidence to the contrary. And we remember this best when we're dwelling

in the secret place, where we focus on truth, not facts. The facts, whether they're in the form of a bank statement, a medical diagnosis, or some other "official" documentation—may be unsettling, unnerving, and downright scary. But one look at the truth will put us on our way back to peace and stability.

Cast Off the Mindset of Lack

Some people don't have peace even in seasons of abundance because their minds are stuck in the memory of an earlier season of lack. You often see this in those who lived during the Great Depression or were raised by parents who remember that period in history. Someone with a "depression" mindset uses the same piece of aluminum foil fifteen times because he doesn't want to be wasteful. No we don't want to be wasteful, yet God wants us to enjoy our season of blessings.

When we are in a season of lack, another key to seeing the season of blessing approach is sowing. We can actually sow our way out of the season of lack. That's what God did for me, and He will do it for you, too. The Lord taught me to be very frugal in my spending and very generous in my giving. He rewards those who give faithfully to the work of His kingdom, as we read in Malachi 3:10:

> *"Bring the whole tithe into the storehouse, that there may be food in my house. Test me in this," says the LORD Almighty, "and see if I will not throw open the floodgates of heaven and pour out so much blessing that you will not have room enough for it."*

Contentment for Every Season

The next key we'll discuss for surviving every financial season also comes from the apostle Paul. He wrote,

69

I know what it is to be in need, and I know what it is to have plenty. I have learned the secret of being content in any and every situation, whether well fed or hungry, whether living in plenty or in want. I can do everything through him who gives me strength (Philippians 4:12-13).

Paul's secret to contentment was relying on God for strength. He didn't say he could weather the financial seasons of life on his own; he said that he could *"do everything,"* including thrive in times of plenty and want, because he leaned on the Lord for strength. We have the same option today. God will give us the strength and the grace we need to endure every financial season, if only we'll lean on Him.

When we are faced with challenging circumstances, again, we need to realize that they are temporary. One night, I was sitting on my floor crying because I was so overwhelmed with the financial responsibilities of being a single mom, coupled with the stress of providing constant care to a newborn. That night, God clearly spoke to me and said, "This is temporary." When something is temporary, it is not permanent. The experiences and circumstances we encounter are often painful and too perplexing to understand. If nothing else, we know at least this much: Those circumstances are temporary. The Lord was basically saying to me, "This is only a season—a temporary season." Just as winter is always followed by spring, *"weeping may endure for a night, but joy comes in the morning"* (Ps. 30:5 NKJV).

There is a time for everything, and a season for every activity under heaven: a time to be born and a time to die, a time to plant and a time to uproot, a time to kill and a time to heal, a time to tear down and a time to build, a time to weep and a time to laugh, a time to mourn and a time to dance, a time to scatter stones and a time to gather them, a time to embrace and a time to refrain, a time to search and a time to give up, a time to keep and a time to throw away, a time to tear and a

*time to mend, a time to be silent and a time to speak, a time
to love and a time to hate, a time for war and a time for peace*
(Ecclesiastes 3:1-8).

The seasons of life are always changing. And so, even in the
cold, blinding blizzards of life, we can take courage and follow
Paul's instructions in Second Corinthians 4:18: *"So we fix our eyes
not on what is seen, but on what is unseen. For what is seen is temporary, but what is unseen is eternal."* When we fix our eyes on the
unseen, we rise above our current, temporary circumstances. And
doing so is a step of faith, which the writer defined as *"being sure
of what we hope for and certain of what we do not see"* (Heb. 11:1).

Today, my financial situation has improved significantly. The
overwhelming circumstances we were experiencing were indeed
temporary, just as God had told me, and what I learned during
that season of life I now apply to every other area in which I'm
faced with a challenge. I've learned to put up my hand and say,
"Temporary!"

Yes, sometimes life is hard, but God is always good. *"We
are hard pressed on every side, but not crushed; perplexed, but not in
despair; persecuted, but not abandoned; struck down, but not destroyed"*
(2 Cor. 4:8-9). My translation of this passage is as follows: "Things
are hard, but they could be a whole lot worse." Yes, we are hard
pressed, but we aren't crushed. We are persecuted, but we aren't
abandoned. We are struck down, but—be encouraged—we aren't
destroyed! Life is hard, but God is good. The hard times we face
can always be worse, and they're only temporary.

You Will Always Have Reason to Rejoice

The storms of life expose what's in our hearts more effectively
than the seasons of peace do. Sometimes what we find out about
ourselves is scary! This is because times of stress and struggle bring
out the attitudes that reside in our hearts. God wants us to have

an attitude of gratitude at all times, storm or no storm. As we are crossing over from the land of "not enough" to the land of "more than enough," God wants us to maintain an attitude of gratitude every step of the way. We are to *give thanks in all circumstances, for this is God's will for you in Christ Jesus*" (1 Thess. 5:18).

The psalmist exemplified an attitude of gratitude, always focusing on what the Lord had done for him. Consider the following passage as an example:

> *Praise the LORD, O my soul, and forget not all his benefits— who forgives all your sins and heals all your diseases, who redeems your life from the pit and crowns you with love and compassion, who satisfies your desires with good things so that your youth is renewed like the eagle's* (Psalm 103:2-5).

The children of Israel, who wandered in the wilderness for forty years, failed to realize that their time in the desert was temporary. One little trial caused them to lose their vision for the Promised Land. Some minor discomfort to their flesh caused them to lose sight of the fact that their temporary circumstances were leading them to the next season of life—the land of more than enough.

Our attitude in the wilderness will determine how long we stay there. I mentioned before that the children of Israel could have made the trip into the Promised Land in just eleven days. But because of their lousy attitude, it took them forty years to get there! We must maintain an attitude of gratitude instead of an attitude that ends up prolonging our seasons in the desert. All of us will go through "desert seasons." Some of us will make the trip in eleven days, others in forty years, and still others will "die" in the desert, never making it to the Promised Land. Make the most of the season that you are in by maintaining an attitude of gratitude. We can even enjoy the wilderness when we realize it's temporary. That way we won't spend any more time than necessary in the wilderness.

CULTIVATE AN ATTITUDE OF GRATITUDE

God won't promote you above the potential of your character. If you have a bad attitude, it will stunt your growth! First Kings 11:11 says,

> *So the LORD said to Solomon, "Since this is your attitude and you have not kept my covenant and my decrees, which I commanded you, I will most certainly tear the kingdom away from you and give it to one of your subordinates."*

Promotion comes from the Lord, and it comes only after you have kept a right heart attitude.

The psalmist asked God to give him a godly attitude when he prayed, *"May the words of my mouth and the meditation of my heart be pleasing in your sight, O LORD, my Rock and my Redeemer"* (Ps. 19:14). We must guard the words of our mouths and the meditations of our hearts, and we have a number of ways to do this.

SPEND TIME IN GOD'S WORD

One of the best methods to maintain a godly "attitude of gratitude" is by studying the Word of God on a daily basis. Reading the Word will reveal to us any impure heart attitudes. As the writer of Hebrews said,

> *For the Word of God is living and active. Sharper than any double-edged sword, it penetrates even to dividing soul and spirit, joints and marrow; it judges the thoughts and attitudes of the heart* (Hebrews 4:12).

If we discover an attitude that doesn't belong in our hearts, our response should involve humble repentance, which the Lord will reward.

PRAISE AND WORSHIP GOD

Colossians 3:16 says,

Let the word of Christ dwell in you richly as you teach and admonish one another with all wisdom, and as you sing psalms, hymns, and spiritual songs with gratitude in your hearts to God.

When we sing and worship God, it cultivates an attitude of gratitude in our hearts toward Him. During the storms of life, if we just keep worshiping, if we just keep praising God for all that we do have, it takes the focus off of what we are lacking and puts it on what He has already given us.

LITTLE KEYS TO ABUNDANT PROVISION

Key #4: Cultivate an attitude of gratitude.

QUESTIONS FOR REFLECTION AND PERSONAL APPLICATION

1. How would you classify the financial season you're experiencing right now?

2. Think back to a season of abundance. Can you see the handprint of God on the blessings you received in that season?

3. When you face a difficult situation, do you tend to operate based on the facts or based on what the Word of God says? How does this affect your ability to weather the storms of life?

4. Would you consider yourself a grateful person? Whether you would or not, everyone could stand to cultivate a more consistent "attitude of gratitude." The next time you're tempted to complain or cry, step back and look for something to be thankful for. Then see how your mindset changes.

Prayer

Ask God to open your eyes to all of the blessings He has given you and all of the reasons you have to be thankful. Then start thanking Him!

CHAPTER 5

"THERE'S A LOT YOU CAN DO WITH A LITTLE FAITH"

[Jesus said,] ..."I tell you the truth, if you have faith as small as a mustard seed, you can say to this mountain, 'Move from here to there' and it will move. Nothing will be impossible for you."

—Matthew 17:20

The opposite of fear is faith. And faith is a key to the miraculous, no matter what kind of miracle you need—a money miracle, a miracle healing, a miracle job, and so forth. Faith takes us to the next level. When God is calling you to a higher level, it will require you to do something you've never done before—and usually it will demand a deeper level of faith.

All too often, we do what I call "getting stuck on the steps." When you get stuck on the steps, you get comfortable and kick back. You think, *I'm going to take a little break. I've had it hard lately. I deserve to rest for a while.* Remember, God is a God of process, and when we get tired of climbing the steps He has set before us, we can get stuck at a place that wasn't supposed to be our final destination.

"But the just shall live by faith…and if [My servant] *draws back and shrinks in fear, My soul has no delight or pleasure in him"* (Heb. 10:38 AMP). Again, faith and fear are often opposites. We must combat the doubts that the enemy throws our way, and we must face our fears. When you face your fears, you can build your faith! If you refuse to face your fears, you will never conquer them, and you will stunt the growth of your faith.

Acquire a New Level of Faith

The Lord not only wants you to have faith, but He wants you to have great faith. Great faith knows that Jesus only has to say the Word. The centurion had *"great faith"*:

The centurion heard of Jesus and sent some elders of the Jews to him, asking him to come and heal his servant. When they came to Jesus, they pleaded earnestly with him, "This man deserves to have you do this, because he loves our nation and has built our synagogue." So Jesus went with them. He was not far from the house when the centurion sent friends to say to him. "Lord, don't trouble yourself, for I do not deserve to have you come under my roof. That is why I did not even consider myself worthy to come to you. But say the word, and my servant will be healed. For I myself am a man under authority, with soldiers under me. I tell this one, 'Go,' and he goes; and that one, 'Come,' and he comes. I say to my servant, 'Do this,' and he does it." When Jesus heard this, he was amazed at him, and turning to the crowd following him, he said, "I tell you, I have not found such great faith even in Israel" (Luke 7:3-9).

Great faith knows that no one has to lay hands on you—except the Holy Spirit. Great faith knows that your miracle does not depend on the strength or abilities of a man or a woman. Great faith knows it's the name of Jesus, and His name alone, that brings about the miraculous. Great faith prays in the name of Jesus and expects results. It was great faith in the name of Jesus that healed the crippled beggar in Acts 3 and made him strong. And it's great faith in the name of Jesus that brings about your provision and the financial miracle that you desperately need today.

Faith Is Built by the Word of God and Words from God

How do we get faith? *"Faith comes by hearing, and hearing by the word of God"* (Rom. 10:17 NKJV). The *"word of God"* refers to both God's written Word—the Holy Bible—and His *rhema* words, or the messages He speaks to our hearts through His Holy Spirit. (His *rhema* word will always line up with His written Word; they cannot contradict each other.) It was a *rhema* word that God spoke to me when He told me about the "little keys" to the miraculous. But that *rhema* word agreed with the written Word—the scriptural truths recorded in the Bible. So as we hear God's Word, faith rises up and grows within our hearts.

It's important to remember that while faith comes by hearing, so does doubt. A spirit of worry and skepticism takes root in our hearts when we hear and dwell on the words of others, including the devil, that don't line up with God's Word. It's crucial that we take such thoughts captive and make them obedient to the Word of the Lord (see 2 Cor. 10:5). If we fail to do this, those words become thoughts that fill our minds and cause us to think, speak, and act out of doubt, not faith.

79

FAITH IS BUILT BY REMEMBERING GOD'S FAITHFULNESS

Our faith increases when we go through situations and circumstances that test our faith. It's not fun, but it does work! Your faith grows during those testing times. We increase in our faith by remembering all that the Lord has done for us in the past. As the vast army came against Jehoshaphat, he prayed and remembered all the times that God had brought him through before. As he reminded himself of God's faithfulness in the past, faith rose up in him.

That faith-boosting technique still works today! I use it all the time. When I receive ministry bills that are much bigger than our bank account can accommodate, I first tell God that He has mail, and then I remind myself of all the other times He has brought us through. God has never failed to take care of His mail, and He's never paid a bill late. He's always provided food for my daughter and me, diapers when Destiny was a baby, and money to pay my mortgage and electric bills, even when all of the evidence pointed to empty pockets. Every time it's looked like the end, God came through, and I know He will do it again and again and again! But I couldn't feel so sure unless I had come through each of those "close calls" and uncomfortable realizations that we were out of money.

GOD'S PROMISES ARE YOURS FOR THE TAKING

Joshua 21:43 says, *"So the LORD gave Israel all the land he had sworn to give their forefathers, and they took possession of it and settled there."* When God promises us something, it's as good as ours, but we have a part to play: We have to possess it. We can't just sit back and wait for it to fall into our laps. When we do that, the enemy sneaks in with his distractions and discouragement. Claim

80

your inheritance in God, and you will see His promises fulfilled in your life. Joshua 21:45 says, *"Not one of all the LORD's good promises to the house of Israel failed; every one was fulfilled."* And the same will be true for you, if you will only seize the promises of God and not doubt.

FAITH TRUMPS FACTS

The antidote to doubt is faith, or perceiving the truth—God's Word—which always trumps the facts in the natural realm. For example, your bank account may say that you only have $10— that's the fact. But the truth is what the Word says. For example, Philippians 4:19 says, *"My God shall supply all your need according to His riches in glory by Christ Jesus"* (NKJV). As long as you are living according to God's principles—tithing, giving, and so forth—then you can stand on His promises. And His promise for your provision always outweighs the facts—whatever your financial situation looks like in the natural realm.

I love how the Amplified Version translates Hebrews 11:1:

Now faith is the assurance (the confirmation, the title deed) of the things [we] hope for, being the proof of things [we] do not see and the conviction of their reality [faith perceiving as real fact what is not revealed to the senses].

Your faith truly is your "title deed" to all of God's promises. Faith truly is a key to the miraculous. What is faith? Faith is hoping in the truth and not losing hope when facing the facts. Abraham is the perfect example of that.

Romans 4:18-21 says,

Against all hope, Abraham in hope believed and so became the father of many nations, just as it had been said to him, "so shall your offspring be." Without weakening in his faith, he faced the fact that his body was as good as dead—since he was about a hundred years old—and that Sarah's womb was also dead. Yet he did not waver through unbelief regarding the promise of God, but was strengthened in his faith and gave glory to God, being fully persuaded that God had power to do what he had promised.

What is faith? Again, faith is being fully persuaded that God has the power to do whatever He has said He's going to do! Faith is being sure of what you hope for and 100 percent certain that it will come to pass, no matter what you see happening in the natural realm right now. What it boils down to is this: Faith knows that God has all the power to do whatever He wants to do, however and whenever He wants to do it!

Are you fully persuaded that God can do and will do what He promised you? Or are you partially persuaded sometimes and not persuaded at all other times?

FAITH FUELS BOLD DETERMINATION TO ACT

James 1:2-3 says that the testing of our faith develops our perseverance, which is almost synonymous with "determination." As our faith is tested and proven, it develops our perseverance into bold determination.

A few days later, when Jesus again entered Capernaum, the people heard that he had come home. So many gathered that there was no room left, not even outside the door, and he preached the word to them. Some men came, bringing to him a paralytic, carried by four of them. Since they could not get him to Jesus because of the crowd, they made an opening in the roof above Jesus and, after digging through it, lowered the mat the paralyzed man was lying on. When Jesus saw their faith, he said to the paralytic, "Son, your sins are forgiven...get up, take your mat and walk" (Mark 2:1-9).

Talk about bold determination! Their bold determination had its foundation in their faith, and Jesus saw their act as evidence of their faith. When Jesus sees our faith, He responds. When God sees our faith, He is moved.

Many years ago, I was lying in bed crying as I poured out my heart to God. I was extremely emotional as I explained to Him why I needed Him to act on my behalf—immediately! He responded with a clear answer in my spirit: "I'm not moved by your emotions; I'm moved by your faith."

When He told me He was moved by my faith alone, I snapped out of it. I stopped praying prayers of self-pity and other emotions, and I started praying bold prayers of declaration. I would proclaim out loud, "God, I thank You that You are going to meet all of my needs. I thank You that You have always come through for me. Thank You that I'm standing on Your Word and on Your promises." As I prayed that way, faith rose up in me, and I immediately felt better. Pretty soon, I was no longer overtaken by my own emotions! Doubt says, "Maybe God will bring me through," but faith says, "Of course, God is going to do it. Of course, God is going to hear my prayers and answer them. Of course!"

Faith Means that "Nothing Will Be Impossible for You"

Jesus said,

Because you have so little faith. I tell you the truth, if you have faith as small as a mustard seed, you can say to this mountain, 'Move from here to there' and it will move. Nothing will be impossible for you (Matthew 17:20-21).

Nothing is impossible for us if we use our faith. The first thing we need to do with our faith is to exercise it. Pray regularly and rely on the Word for the content of your prayers. As you sow your seed of faith, you will see it grow—it really is amazing!

If you can move a mountain with a little seed of faith, imagine what you can do after you have exercised your faith. Imagine what you can do after you allow the Holy Spirit to supersize your faith. All the tests and trials you have been through, they are really the hand of God sprinkling some Miracle Gro on your faith. Before you know it, your faith will be supersized! And then it will be time to put it to use at a level like never before.

What do we do with our faith? We add works to it! You can have all the faith in the world, but if you don't step out of the boat, you will never walk on the water. Kim Clement prophesied over me years ago that God was going to open my womb and that I was going to conceive a little girl. When I heard this, I was so excited, and my faith for this particular event rose up in me. But I needed to add some works to my faith that came from hearing the Word. There wasn't going to be another virgin birth! So I had to take my faith and add some works (my part) to it. James 2:26 says, *"As the body without the spirit is dead, so faith without deeds is dead."* My faith would be dead if I didn't add some works, or action, to it. I won't elaborate any further. If you don't get it, go ask your mother—or someone's mother—to explain it to you.

FAITH COMPELS US

When we have faith, we do great things for God as we follow His leading, just like Noah did. God told him to build an ark, and He gave him some seriously specific details that sounded illogical to most everyone Noah knew (see Gen. 6). Yet *"Noah did every-thing just as God commanded him"* (see Gen. 6:22). His faith—and faithfulness—were recognized by the author of Hebrews in his Faith Hall of Fame:

[Prompted] by faith Noah, being forewarned by God concerning events of which as yet there was no visible sign, took heed and diligently and reverently constructed and prepared an ark for the deliverance of his own family... (Hebrews 11:7 AMP).

Faith will prompt you to do things way out of your comfort zone. Remember, it had never rained before! All of his neighbors thought Noah was crazy. There were probably even days when Noah questioned his own sanity.

Faith will prompt you to do great things for God, as long as you yield to the prompting of the Holy Spirit. Don't stop at your current faith level, but keep going forward, ever pressing to the next level of faith to which the Lord is calling you.

Like Noah, Abraham was a man spurred forward by faith. Hebrews 11:8 says,

[Urged on] by faith Abraham, when he was called, obeyed and went forth to a place which he was destined to receive as an inheritance; and he went, although he did not know or trouble his mind about where he was to go (AMP).

Don't try to talk yourself out of anything your faith is prompting you to do. Just go for it! Surround yourself with those who are in agreement with you and your faith, because there's great power in agreement! Don't "trouble" your mind or worry about where you are going as you follow the leading and prompting of your faith.

Hebrews 11:6 says that it is impossible for us to please God if we don't have faith. It's our faith that prompts us to walk in obedience to the leading of the Holy Spirit, and this brings great pleasure to God. It takes faith to do what God tells you to do—to respond to His "illogical" instructions by getting out of the boat and walking on water (see Matt. 14:22-29) or speaking to a mountain and telling it to move (see Matt. 17:20; 21:21; Mark 11:23).

Even if everyone around you is telling you to give up your faith and quit pestering God, go for it! That's what blind Bartimaeus did. He refused to stop asking God in faith for a miracle, despite those around him who tried to silence him.

> *As Jesus and his disciples, together with a large crowd, were leaving the city [Jericho], a blind man, Bartimaeus (that is, the Son of Timaeus), was sitting by the roadside begging. When he heard that it was Jesus of Nazareth, he began to shout, "Jesus, Son of David, have mercy on me!" Many rebuked him and told him to be quiet, but he shouted all the more, "Son of David, have mercy on me!" Jesus stopped and said, "Call him." So they called to the blind man, "Cheer up! On your feet! He's calling you." Throwing his cloak aside, he jumped to his feet and came to Jesus. "What do you want me to do for you?" Jesus asked him. The blind man said, "Rabbi, I want to see." "Go," said Jesus, "your faith has healed you." Immediately he received his sight and followed Jesus along the road* (Mark 10:46-52).

Faith in God lets you expect big things from Him. Expect Him to do the extraordinary for you!

ELIMINATING OBSTACLES TO FAITH

Jesus said to His disciples, *"If you have faith as small as a mustard seed, you can say to this mountain, 'Move from here to there' and it will move. Nothing will be impossible for you"* (Matt. 17:20-21). Anything is possible if you have faith. What are you doing with your measure? Ephesians 3:20 says, *"Now to him who is able to do immeasurably more than all we ask or imagine, according to his power that is at work within us."* Father is able to do more than you are asking and imagining. Your faith releases Him to do just that. But if you withhold your faith from Him, God is bound by those limits. Stop tying His hands! Through faith, loosen any limits you've been placing on God. Then sit back and get ready for a miracle!

CAST OUT THE DOUBT

Doubt causes our dreams and visions to die. Doubt causes marriages and relationships to die. Doubt causes abilities to die. If you doubt your abilities instead of trusting God to work through you, you may never come into your full potential. Doubt causes all kinds of things to die. But the good news is that God is in the business of resurrecting dead stuff! After all, Jesus said that He came to give us abundant life (see John 10:10 NKJV). Allow the Lord to resurrect and give life to those areas that Satan has tried to kill with doubt! God has given each of us *"a measure of faith"* (Rom. 12:3 NKJV). Your measure can be a "big scoop" if you'll only exercise your faith and let it grow.

MAKE POSITIVE CONFESSIONS

When I was in college, a lot of my fellow students would go out to dinner during the week at nice restaurants, and then on the weekends, they would travel to other cities—even out of state—to attend Christian conferences. My experience was a lot different. First of all, when I was growing up, we rarely went out to dinner. We might have stopped at McDonald's a time or two, but I have no memories from childhood of restaurant dinners. Our family budget didn't allow for restaurant dining; plus, we lived on a farm and raised a lot of our own food, so we mostly cooked at home.

One day, some of my college friends announced that they were going to Tulsa, Oklahoma, for a conference. I immediately said, "I will never have the money to do that." Right after I had spoken those words, the Holy Spirit said something that really shook me: "You never will have the money if you keep saying you won't." That was the first time I realized the power of spoken words.

The experience totally changed the way that I spoke from that day forward. I started saying things like, "Lord, I thank You that

You give me enough money to do everything that You want me to do and to go everywhere You want me to go." Not long after that, I had enough money to travel to Christian conferences in Tulsa and elsewhere.

It's true that *"death and life are in the power of the tongue"* (Prov. 18:21 NKJV). There is a miracle in your mouth that's just waiting to come out, but you have to speak the right words—words of positive faith in God's ability to meet your needs.

> *Now Jericho was tightly shut up because of the Israelites. No one went out and no one came in. Then the LORD said to Joshua, "See, I have delivered Jericho into your hands, along with its king and its fighting men. March around the city once with all the armed men. Do this for six days. Have seven priests carry trumpets of rams' horns in front of the ark. On the seventh day, march around the city seven times, with the priests blowing the trumpets. When you hear them sound a long blast on the trumpets, have all the people give a loud shout; then the wall of the city will collapse and the people will go up, every man straight in"* (Joshua 6:1-5).

Sometimes, we have to "shout out the doubt" in order to press our way into the miraculous. When we learn to shout out the doubt, we can go forward and take the ground that God has given us. Doubt and fear form a wall that we must tear down through our words if we expect to possess the miracles God has for us.

Maybe you doubt you will ever experience financial freedom. Maybe you doubt you will ever be free from debt. Go ahead and shout those walls of doubt right down! When my daughter was an infant, I often didn't know how I was going to afford more diapers or enough baby food. Whenever this happened, God would often tell me to shout. So I would walk around my little house, shouting praise and glory to God and proclaiming at the top of my lungs

that He would supply all my needs. Shouting causes joy and victory to rise up in your spirit, just as it did for Joshua.

Your place today is the same. Walk in obedience to the voice of the Lord and go ahead and shout those walls of debt right down! Never doubt God's ability to eliminate your debt and take care of you financially.

Jesus said,

I tell you the truth, if anyone says to this mountain, 'Go, throw yourself into the sea,' and does not doubt in his heart but believes that what he says will happen, it will be done for him (Mark 11:23).

The problem is that we doubt in our hearts! We get the doubt out by shouting it out. We get the doubt out by taking control of our minds as we bring every thought captive to the Word of God. We get the doubt out by tuning out other people's words. Words are like seeds. Don't allow negative seeds that are contrary to the Word of God to take root in your heart.

WHAT YOU SEE IS WHAT YOU GET

If you think this season is your final destination, it probably will be, because perception precedes possession. If you can't see yourself out of poverty, chances are you will remain impoverished. If you can't see yourself free from debt, chances are you never will be. Unless you put on your "spiritual eyes" and see yourself healed and whole, you will remain sick and broken. We must see it, reach for it, and then possess all of the promises God has for every realm of our lives.

You have to see yourself blessed and prosperous, and that's a very important way that you prepare for your future season of abundance—you must see it! In Genesis 13:14-15, the Lord said to Abraham, *"Lift up your eyes from where you are and look north and south, east and west. All the land that you see I will give to you and your offspring forever.*" God said, "Okay. What you can see, I will give you." Abraham had to see it before he could possess it, and the same is true for us. If we can't see ourselves living in a season of abundance, we will probably never make it to the land of more than enough. But if we can see it, God will give it to us, because He desires to shower us with abundant blessings!

During the days of extreme lack as a single mom, I had to envision myself on the other side of my current season. The fact is, I was believing God for each diaper and every jar of baby food— daily! But I was determined that my faith was going to change the facts and transform my financial situation. The Lord kept telling me that I needed to "see" myself in a place of abundance. Now, when you have been living on corn dogs and tuna fish for eighteen months, it's a little challenging to see the pathway out of the wilderness and on to the Promised Land. But that's where obedience came into play for me. The Lord put it on my heart to go to the nicest mall in our community to window shop. I would treat myself to a chocolate bar and walk around saying, "Thank You, Lord, that the day is coming when I will be able to come to this mall and buy anything I want." At the time, it seemed crazy, because I didn't have more than $20 to last me until the end of the month. But I needed to see myself, through faith, in a place of blessing. The atmosphere of the mall gave me a different picture from my surroundings at home, where the cupboards were bare and even the toilet paper had to be rationed.

I am happy to report that I now could shop at the mall on a regular basis, if I chose to. I am always frugal with my spending, so I don't go on shopping sprees, but if I truly need something, to obtain it is no longer a major obstacle, praise God. If we hang on to hope and refuse to park in the pit of lack, the shift in our financial season will be right around the corner.

Compromise Blurs Your Vision

Genesis 13:14-15 says,

The LORD said to Abram after Lot had parted from him, "Lift up your eyes from where you are and look north and south, east and west. All the land that you see I will give to you and your offspring forever."

Until Abram parted ways with his nephew Lot, he could not see clearly all that the Lord had for him. The reason was that Lot represented sin and compromise. When we put up with sin and compromise instead of "parting ways" with them, our vision is blurred, and we're unable to set our sights on the destinies to which God is calling us.

Leave a Legacy of Faith

Noah, Abraham, and so many others left a legacy of faith that still inspires us today. God wants us to follow in their footsteps and leave our own legacy of faith for those who come after us.

The Book of Hebrews includes what many people call the Faith Hall of Fame (see Heb. 11:4-30). Here is a summary of the legacy of these faith-filled folks. They were commended for their faith, and the Lord wants the same to be said of us, both today and long after we leave this earth.

By faith...

- Abel offered a better sacrifice than Cain, and God called him righteous (see Heb. 11:4).

- Enoch pleased God, and he was taken from the earth without experiencing death (see Heb. 11:5-6).

- Noah obeyed God's instructions and built an ark (see Heb. 11:7).

- Abraham followed the Lord's leading, and though he was clueless about his final destination, he remained confident that God would bring him an inheritance (see Heb. 11:8-11).

- Abraham and Sarah believed God's promise to give them a son, and they conceived (see Heb. 11:11-12).

- Abraham was prepared to sacrifice his promised son, Isaac, in obedience to the Lord's command (see Heb. 11:17-19).

- Isaac blessed his sons, Jacob and Esau, and entrusted their futures to God (see Heb. 11:20).

- Jacob blessed the sons of his beloved son Joseph (see Heb. 11:21).

- Joseph prophesied about the Israelites' exodus from Egypt (see Heb. 11:22).

- Moses' parents defied the king's edict and hid their infant son so that he would live (see Heb. 11:23).

- Moses led God's people out of Egypt and obeyed Him unswervingly (see Heb. 11:24-28).

- The Israelites passed through the Red Sea when Moses, by the power of God, parted the waters (see Heb. 11:29).

- Joshua led his army around the walls of Jericho seven times and then watched as it crumbled (see Heb. 11:30).

Wow—that's encouraging! Faith can move mountains, both in our own lives and in the lives of our descendants who are inspired by our example. When you exercise great faith and leave a legacy of belief in God, it pleases Him to no end. For further encouragement, read this assurance from Jesus:

I tell you the truth, anyone who has faith in me will do what I have been doing. He will do even greater things than these, because I am going to the Father. And I will do whatever you ask in my name, so that the Son may bring glory to the Father. You may ask me for anything in my name, and I will do it (John 14:12-14).

Grab onto that promise and go for it! God has everything under control. When you trust fully in Him, your faith will work its way to an all-time high. Just think of the mountains you'll move!

LITTLE KEYS TO ABUNDANT PROVISION

Key #5: Shout out the doubt!

QUESTIONS FOR REFLECTION AND PERSONAL APPLICATION

1. Think about a time when God came through for you or someone you know in a miraculous way. Then whenever you're facing a seemingly impossible situation, call to mind that particular instance. What is the effect on your mindset and faith level?

2. Has God ever given you instructions that sounded illogical? How did you respond? Has reading this chapter changed your mind about how you'll respond to "illogical" instructions in the future?

3. Pay attention to the words you speak in regard to your finances. Are they mostly positive or negative? Make a conscious effort to speak only words of faith and see what happens.

Prayer

Thank the Lord for all of the times He has provided for you in the past, and then proclaim your faith in His ability to come through for you again and again. Ask Him to give you a *rhema* word that will build your faith in His provision.

CHAPTER 6

"I WILL BLESS YOUR OBEDIENCE"

*I will surely bless you and make your descendants as
numerous as the stars in the sky and as the sand on
the seashore...and through your offspring all nations
on earth will be blessed, because you have obeyed me.*

—Genesis 22:17-18

[Jesus said], *"Blessed...are those who hear the word of
God and obey it."*

—Luke 11:28

Several years ago, I was saving up for a new vehicle. My van
was very old, and although it was paid off, the repairs it needed
were starting to add up. I sensed that it was time for a new vehicle. Yet, as soon as I would get a little stash of money saved the
Lord would give me illogical instructions, such as, "I want you
to give that little stash to this person or that ministry." This happened several times, and it was always difficult for me to part with

my hard-earned cash. Plus, wouldn't you know it, my van would require another costly repair. More than once, my air conditioner broke just days after I'd kissed another "nest egg" good-bye. Of course, that happened on some of the hottest days of the year! I was left driving around with no air conditioner and a fear that I'd lost my mind. I would think, *Most normal people save their money and go buy a new car, but not me!*

OBEY EVEN ILLOGICAL INSTRUCTIONS

I have since learned that illogical instructions often lead to miracles! Think about the man with the withered hand whose story is told in chapter 12 of Matthew and chapter 3 of Mark. Jesus told him to stretch out his hand toward Him, and He would heal him. I can imagine the man saying, "Well, if I could stretch out my hand, I wouldn't need a miracle, now, would I?" It seemed so illogical, but it was the very command that brought about his miracle.

Meanwhile, God was doing a great work in my heart. He was teaching me immediate, total obedience. Delayed obedience is not obedience; it's really repentance. But it's better to repent and then obey than to be stiff-necked and refuse to obey the Holy Spirit at all. Proverbs 29:1 says, *"A man who remains stiff-necked after many rebukes will suddenly be destroyed—without remedy."* We risk self-destructing through our own disobedience, to the devastation of our financial futures, our family futures, and even our very lives, if we are stiff-necked and ignore the Holy Spirit's commands.

OBEY AND RECEIVE

As the Lord whispered in my heart that I should give away my stash, He also whispered, "I'm going to give you a car." There are so many things that the Lord wants to give us, if only we

will trust Him and walk by faith. This requires us to stop trying to earn everything on our own, including our miracles. God wants to give you a miracle. Maybe you need a miracle of physical healing. Maybe the miracle you need is in the area of finances. Regardless of what type, a miracle is what God has in store for you. You don't have to work for it or try to earn it. All you need to do is walk in obedience. Yes, the Lord requires us to work—if we want to eat, that is (see 2 Thess. 3:10). As a matter of fact, after God created Adam, the first thing He gave him was a job. He placed Adam in the Garden and said, "Get to work" (see Gen. 2:15). Adam had a job before he had a wife. I think we ought to follow God's order of things. No young man had better come and ask for my daughter's hand in marriage unless he has a job that can support the two of them! So, yes, we work, and we work hard, but we also work hard at walking in obedience to God and maintaining total trust in Him.

Obey Patiently as You Await Your Miracle

God finally gave me my new car—two long years later! I had just returned from several speaking engagements, and I was catching up on emails and phone messages with my administrative assistant, when she handed me a stack of papers to look through. I glanced at the paper on the top of the stack and couldn't believe my eyes. I read it two or three times to make sure I wasn't mistaken. Then I shouted, "Rebekah!" My assistant came running into my office to see what the problem was.

There wasn't a problem—there was a *solution* to my long-standing problem! I asked her if she had read the message on top, and she replied, "No, why?" I read it aloud to her, and her eyes grew as big as mine: "I have done some research according to your zip code and found your local Lexus dealer. Have Danette go and pick out what she wants and make sure she gets a 100,000-mile complete warranty. Just let me know the price, and I'll wire her the money."

My first response was, "Is this a joke? Who is this guy?" What a show of a great woman of faith, right? Then I said, "Do we have his phone number? Get this guy on the phone."

The car dealership that was mentioned in the email was the same dealer I had visited one year prior, when the Lord had told me to go pick out the car I wanted. I had started at the local Toyota dealership, but the Highlander was too small for my needs, and the Sequoia was too big. A few days later, after finding out from a friend that Lexus and Toyota are made by the same company, I stopped by the Lexus dealer. It didn't take me long to find what I wanted, and I left with a smile on my face and the salesman's business card in my hand. I had told the salesman that God was going to do a miracle for me and that I would be back to get my car as soon as my miracle manifested. He had a strange look on his face, despite his best efforts to hide it!

One week before my miraculous email arrived, I had been cleaning out my purse, and I'd come across the business card of the Lexus salesman. I was about to give up on my miracle and nearly threw it in the trash. But as my hand held it suspended over the wastebasket, a divine nudge told me to hang on to the card just a little while longer. I have since learned that if we just hang on a little while longer, our miracle will be right around the corner!

Rebekah reached the gentleman by phone and put him through to me. I told him that I had already picked out the vehicle I wanted at the very dealership he had mentioned, and I gave him the name of the salesman. He instructed me to go to the dealership immediately and fax him a copy of the invoice.

When I left my office at the end of the day, I picked up Destiny at school and headed straight for the dealership. Recalling the strange look on the face of the salesman one year earlier, I decided

to park my sputtering, rattling, squeaking van in a remote corner of the lot, far out of sight. After all, I wanted the salesman to take me seriously when I told him someone would be wiring him the money for my new vehicle. We got out of the car and approached the showroom, our excitement mounting. When we opened the door and entered the showroom, both of us were overwhelmed at the sight of all of the beautiful new vehicles on display. I managed to maintain my composure, again wanting to be taken seriously. But not Destiny. She blurted out, "Wow, Mom! These cars are really nice—they don't even have any dents in them!" I blushed in embarrassment as my daughter's voice echoed around the show-room, expressing the very thoughts I was keeping a secret.

The salesman greeted us and took us to see the model I had picked out the previous year. "That's it!" I said. "That's the one I want." Not only did I get the exact vehicle I wanted, but I got the newer model that had just come out. I asked him to write up the invoice, including a 100,000-mile extended warranty. When he returned, I reviewed the invoice and informed him that someone would be wiring him the money in the morning. I then asked if I could drive the vehicle home that night.

I thought he was going to choke! He said, "Oh no, Mrs. Crawford. We never allow that." I assured him that I understood and promised to come back the next day, after the wire transfer, to pick up my new Lexus. Once again, his face bore one of the most baffled expressions I have ever seen. I could tell that he didn't believe a word I had said, and I knew he thought he had just wasted several hours of his time.

The next evening, Destiny and I showed up at the dealership with a check in hand. I thought our salesman was going to pass out! Needless to say, I had a captive audience, so I took full advantage of the opportunity. A couple of his coworkers came out of the back room to meet me—evidently, I had become a legend around there. It was a fantastic opportunity to witness to them, and one salesman even recommitted his life to the Lord after several years of backsliding. Another salesperson informed me that his father was a pastor, and though he'd grown up going to church, he wasn't where he needed to be in his relationship with the Lord. He allowed me to pray with him. I encouraged all of the salespeople that God wanted to give them their miracle, just as He had given me mine in the form of my new Lexus. When they heard about my television show, *Joy in the Morning,* and learned that it was about to be aired, they said that they'd tune in on the television in their break room. This was no coincidence, but a divine setup from the Lord.

OBEDIENCE BRINGS MIRACLES IN DIFFERENT MANNERS

What miracle are you in need of today? Never give up on believing God for your miracle; it's just around the corner, so be encouraged! I have spoken to many people over the years who have said, "I want to get a miracle!" The truth is, you never get a miracle unless you need one. Receiving a miracle is so appealing, but the state of being in need of a miracle is hardly to be envied. And it's also important to remember that we can't expect a miracle if we aren't being obedient to the Lord.

A few years back, I flew out of town to speak at a church, and the woman who met me at the airport to take me to my hotel was driving a Lexus. I told her about my "miracle Lexus." You know the story, but it's worth adding that God told me afterward that He had gotten me out of debt, and that I shouldn't get myself back in debt. I couldn't borrow money and go into debt to get another vehicle, so, I thought, *I'd better start saving up.*

But the Lord was setting the stage for my miracle and working obedience in me all at the same time. As I shared with the lady picking me up from the airport that a stranger had bought me my

Lexus, she said, "I want a miracle like that." She said she was still making payments on hers. I shared with her that she was experiencing her miracle—on a monthly basis! She had a job, she was making her payments on time, and God was blessing her. To her, my miracle seemed more exciting, but I informed her that living through the days—the years, actually—leading up to my miracle had been far from thrilling. We love to get miracles, but we never like to be in the place where we need one. No matter what season you are in today, be encouraged—if you have a need, God has a miracle with your name on it.

Pass the Test of Obedience

God is a God of process and order. He does things line upon line, precept upon precept. We never just step into anything that He has for us. God, out of His great love for us, prepares us even when we don't know that we are being prepared or why. An important part of God's preparation process is the tests He administers to us—especially the test of obedience. And because He loves us so much, He never allows us to fail, but generously offers us as many retakes as we need.

Isaiah 1:19 says, *"If you are willing and obedient, you will eat the best from the land."* It's clear throughout Scripture that God wants His children—you and me—to have the best. If you are a parent, think of how strongly you desire that your children have the best. Now multiply the strength of that feeling as many times as you can, and you'll get a sense of how strongly our heavenly Father desires to bless us! Whether we receive His blessings is really up to us. We can open or close the door on the blessings of Father God by our choices. Again, the Word assures us of blessings *"if* [we] *are willing and obedient...."* If we get successfully past the *if,* then we have passed the first step! Willingness and obedience are the first two requirements on the road to receiving God's best.

Going all the way is a different matter. Our spirits may be willing, but our flesh may be too weak for us to follow through with true obedience. *"The spirit indeed is willing, but the flesh is weak"* (Matt. 26:41 NKJV; Mark 14:38 NKJV). Sometimes I have gone to the Lord in prayer and said, "Lord, I'm willing to be willing. Please help me over this obstacle, by the power of Your Holy Spirit."

If we are willing, and if we follow through with obedience, then and only then will we eat the best of the land. It's easy to be willing to follow the Lord's guidance; it's much harder to actually obey it. Being willing will take you to a certain level, but obedience will take you all the way into everything Father has for you. God wants to give us the best there is, but He can do so only if we qualify through our obedience to receive it.

NO PROXIES

The thing about the spiritual tests we take is that no one can take the test for us—there are no proxies. Likewise, we can't take the test on another's behalf. It can be difficult to see loved ones in the midst of a test, especially when you think you know the answer. Don't presume to know. Let them seek God's will and pass the test on their own. This is perhaps the hardest when you see your spouse or your son or daughter about to make a big mistake. We can offer guidance in the form of biblical wisdom—God's tests are always open Book! But ultimately, they're the ones who need to pass the test on their own, while we pray for them.

YOU CAN'T OBEY IF YOU DON'T KNOW THE WAY

We must do what God has told us to do. I keep a journal of everything God says to me, and the reason I believe this is so

102

important for all of us is based on the Parable of the Sower in Luke 8:

> *...The seed is the Word of God. Those along the path are the ones who hear, and then the devil comes and takes away the word from their hearts, so that they may not believe and be saved. Those on the rock are the ones who receive the word with joy when they hear it, but they have no root. They believe for a while, but in the time of testing they fall away. The seed that fell among thorns stands for those who hear, but as they go on their way they are choked by life's worries, riches and pleasures, and they do not mature. But the seed on good soil stands for those with a noble and good heart, who hear the word, retain it, and by persevering produce a crop* (Luke 8:11-15).

The enemy comes to immediately steal the Word. He wants us to forget it, not to understand or comprehend or even hear what God is saying. That's why recording His messages to us is crucial. Of course, we also have to obey them so that we avoid being hearers of the Word, but not doers (see James 1:22). That way, we will be sure to know the Father's will for us—His *"good, pleasing and perfect will"* (Rom. 12:2) that always works to prosper His obedient children.

Don't let anyone or anything keep you from obeying God. Galatians 5:7-8 says, *"You were running a good race. Who cut in on you and kept you from obeying the truth? That kind of persuasion does not come from the one who calls you."* God's Word—the truth—is God's instruction book for you.

In Second Chronicles 31:21, it says of King Hezekiah that

> *In everything that he undertook in the service of God's temple and in obedience to the law and the command, he sought his God and worked wholeheartedly. And so he prospered.*

Hezekiah prospered because he obeyed God, sought Him in every endeavor, and worked hard. His prosperity didn't come from observing just one of these keys, but from doing all three. As we seek God about His choices for our lives, as we obey His voice in every area of our lives, and as we work hard to do what He tells us to do, we will prosper!

KNOWING GOD'S WILL VERSUS DOING IT

Years ago, when I was on staff at a large church, a young man would routinely stop by my office and ask me if I thought it was God's will for him to marry the young lady he was dating. The Lord said to me one day, "He already knows My will. I have told him what to do, yet he is coming to you in hopes of getting another answer because he didn't like the answer I gave him."

That's true for a lot of us. We know what God wants us to do, yet we are faced with an obedience test that we really don't want to pass. I'm happy to say that this young man passed the test and was blessed as a result. He ended up marrying a beautiful woman of God, and shortly after their wedding, they were sent out into ministry together.

OBEY GOD, EVEN IF YOU LACK
COMPLETE UNDERSTANDING

God's Word tells us that His will is for us to be blessed going in and blessed going out (see Deut. 28:6). However, we can tie the hands of God by our disobedience. God had great blessings in store for Abraham, but he had to be obedient to go when Father said, "Go!" The Lord will tell you to do things that aren't convenient to your flesh—do them anyway! Father will tell you to do things that seem impossible or don't make any sense in the natural. Go for it; it may be an obedience test. Obedience always brings blessings, while disobedience always grieves the Holy Spirit. Our obedience opens the door for blessings, just as our disobedience ties the hands of God from releasing the blessings He wants to get to us.

If you are a parent, don't you rejoice when your children walk in obedience? Likewise, doesn't it grieve your heart when they disobey you and ignore the things you have taught them? The same is true with our heavenly Father and us—His children. Romans 16:19 says, *"Everyone has heard about your obedience, so I am full of joy over you...."* God rejoices over us when we are obedient, and He gets great joy from it, just as we do when our children obey us.

Obedience always brings about righteousness, and your obedience doesn't just affect you; it also affects others around you. Romans 5:19 says, *"For just as through the disobedience of the one man the many were made sinners, so also through the obedience of the one man the many will be made righteous."* Righteousness means doing the right thing. Obedience always causes us to do, act, say, and think the right things.

Obey God with the Way You Manage Your Resources

Throughout the Bible, we see example after example of people who were rewarded for their obedience. In many cases, obedience is the key to seeing a manifestation of the miraculous. God wants you to follow your budget and obey Him in regard to managing your resources—not only your money, but also your time, your energy, your talents, your physical blessings, and so forth. Money is far from your greatest resource.

The Lord wants us to be obedient to budget all of our resources, including our time and health. Don't let the enemy steal your resources. Don't get "sticky fingers" and try to hang on to your resources, especially if the Holy Spirit is directing you to give a portion of them toward the kingdom of God. It's often more of a struggle to give generously when you've received an increase in resources. For example, it was harder for me to give sacrificially once I had saved a little bit of money than it had been when I didn't have any. I don't understand it, really, but I guess when I didn't have anything, I was so used to walking by faith that it was just an everyday necessity to walk by faith and to respond with immediate obedience.

The same is true with our time. When people retire and have more time, they often seem to have less. I believe that when we aren't required to live on a strict budget, whether it's a budget of money, time, or something else, we become less disciplined and find it harder to give.

We can break free from financial bondage by walking in obedience, which is submission to the will of the Father.

DON'T GET "TESTY" IN THE MIDST OF TESTING

What test are you facing today? Don't get mad at those around you, because they aren't administering the test—God is. The young man I told you about recently admitted to me that he'd known all along what God wanted him to do. He'd also known, deep in his heart, why I would never give him an answer. It's at this point that many people get angry and think it's those around them who are testing them, when God is really the One who's leading them and preparing them for His best.

AVOIDING DISOBEDIENCE

In First Samuel 15:22-23, we read,

...To obey is better than sacrifice, and to heed is better than the fat of rams. For rebellion is like the sin of divination [witchcraft],

106

and arrogance like the evil of idolatry. Because you have rejected the word of the LORD, he has rejected you as king.

Wow—that is strong, but it is the truth! We can lose our anointing because of disobedience. God can and will remove His Spirit and favor from us if we are persistent in our disobedience. We prosper in every way when we obey the Word of the Lord.

Even Partial Obedience Counts as Disobedience

Saul's disobedience caused the Lord to remove His favor from him. Obedience, on the other hand, releases blessing and miracles. We don't have to understand why God is saying to do something; all we need to do is obey. We reap blessings from obedience and curses from disobedience.

Deuteronomy 28:1-2 says,

If you fully obey the LORD your God and carefully follow all his commands I give you today, the LORD your God will set you high above all the nations on earth. All these blessings will come upon you and accompany you if you obey the LORD your God.

That's what I call the "big if"—"If you fully obey," not "if you partially obey." If you fully obey the Lord, you will receive all of His blessings. Yes, our God is a loving Father who blesses us in spite of ourselves, but I want all the blessings He has for me. And receiving *"all these blessings"* requires all of my obedience.

Withstand Temptation to Disobey

Every one of us has to make the choice to stand against temptation. No one else can do it for us. Resisting temptation is an

107

individual choice. If you are facing difficult times financially, you must resist the temptation to take shortcuts, fudge your tax return, embezzle from your employer, and so forth. You don't have to rob a bank to steal—remember, it's the *"little foxes that spoil the vines"* (Song of Sol. 2:15 NKJV). As you remain clothed in the belt of truth, you can successfully withstand any temptation that comes your way.

James 1:14-15 says, *"But each one is tempted when, by his own evil desire, he is dragged away and enticed. Then, after desire has conceived, it gives birth to sin; and sin, when it is full-grown, gives birth to death."* According to the Word, it's our own evil desires that tempt us—not God, not our friends, not our situations. Anytime we fall into temptation, it's because of our own carnal flesh. Likewise, anytime we choose to resist temptation, it has to be our own decision. We must stand for ourselves.

Being tempted is not a sin, but yielding to it is. If you allow yourself to be dragged away and enticed by it, that's sin. If you allow that sin to take place, and you don't repent and stop the sinful behavior, the Word says that it will grow. And when it is full-grown, it brings about death—spiritual, emotional, financial, and even physical death.

You have to choose not to quit. You have to choose not to give in to sin. You have to choose to stand against the temptation to have a mental meltdown. Thankfully, you aren't alone—God will help you, if you'll just ask Him!

First Corinthians 10:13 says,

No temptation has seized you except what is common to man. And God is faithful; he will not let you be tempted beyond what you can bear. But when you are tempted, he will also provide a way out so that you can stand up under it.

Yes, God will give you an out, but you have to be willing to take it. Then, when you call on the name of Jesus, He will show up

with a host of angels to lead you out of those tempting moments. He always provides a way out, but you have to want to get out.

God May Speak Through a Storm

Sometimes God speaks to us through the storms of life, especially if we've been disobedient and have been ignoring His voice. A prime example is Jonah. The Lord had commanded him to go to Nineveh to convict the people of sin, but Jonah didn't feel like it, so he fled to Tarshish, instead.

> *The word of the LORD came to Jonah son of Amittai: "Go to the great city of Nineveh and preach against it, because its wickedness has come up before me." But Jonah ran away from the LORD and headed for Tarshish. He went down to Joppa, where he found a ship bound for that port. After paying the fare, he went aboard and sailed for Tarshish to flee from the LORD* (Jonah 1:1-3).

Before long, Jonah found himself in a huge storm because of his disobedience (see Jonah 1:4-10). He told the crew and passengers on board with him, *"'Pick me up and throw me into the sea,' he replied, 'and it will become calm. I know that it is my fault that this great storm has come upon you'"* (Jonah 1:12).

It's worth noting that Jonah was not the sole person affected by this particular storm. He may have been responsible for it, because of his disobedience, but everybody else onboard the ship was just as terrified as he was. Sometimes, we find ourselves in a storm that was stirred up by our own sin. Other times, it's someone else's folly that brings the wind and the rain. Maybe today, you're riding out a storm that was brought on by someone else's disobedience. If so, be encouraged! God's got their number, and He will bring you all through the storm.

Maybe you are in a storm of your own making. Remember that your disobedience always affects those around you. We're all in the same boat.

The Lord sent a storm in order to get Jonah back into His will. Sometimes we find ourselves in a situation where our ship—or our life—is threatening to break into a million pieces because Father is trying to get us back on track. Jonah still had a choice to make, and he made the right one—he chose to get up out of his mess and go do the right thing.

Yet God did not abandon him to the waves. After Jonah had owned up to the fact that he was responsible for the storm and had voluntarily gone overboard, *"the Lord provided a great fish to swallow Jonah, and Jonah was inside the fish three days and three nights"* (Jonah 1:17). The Lord made provision for Jonah when he decided to get up out of his mess—even in the middle of the a raging storm on the ocean. God always makes miraculous provision for us when we accept responsibility and make the choice to get up out of our mess. No matter how big your mess is today, and no matter how you got there, if you make the choice to get up out of your mess, Father God will hold your hand and gently lead you out, one step at a time.

Maybe you are in a financial mess because you didn't obey God. Or maybe your problems stem from somebody else's disobedience. Regardless of how you got into these circumstances, be willing to hear correction, and God will surely speak to you. He is a God of second chances—and third chances and fourth chances and so on! God gave Jonah a second chance, and he obeyed. You, too, can choose obedience today. Don't keep looking back at your mistakes or the mistakes of others who may have brought a storm upon you. Instead, look forward to the bright day that God has ahead for you.

Even though the raging storm tossed Jonah's ship for a while, both on the ship and inside the fish, he made it back to dry land

to see the sun shine again. Get ready for the sun to begin shinning again on your circumstances. That sunny day is just around the corner!

LITTLE KEYS TO ABUNDANT PROVISION

Key #6: Obey God fully, even if His instructions sound "illogical."

QUESTIONS FOR REFLECTION AND PERSONAL APPLICATION

1. Have you ever waited a long time for a miracle? Were you patient or anxious (or both, at times)? What was the ultimate outcome?

2. When you spend time studying God's Word, the Holy Spirit often reveals fresh insights to you through a *rhema* word. Why is it so important to record any instructions you receive from Him?

3. On a scale of 1 to 5, 1 being "Just Barely" and 5 being "Completely," rate yourself on...

   • Your understanding of God's Word

   • Your willingness to obey God's Word

   • Your track record of knowing *and* doing what God's Word says

4. God spoke to Jonah through a storm—a harrowing experience that ultimately enabled him to get right with God. Have you ever been through a storm of life

after which you heard a message from God? What was it? How did you respond?

Prayer

Thank the Lord for His Word and for illuminating your mind to know what He desires for you to do. Then pray that He would reveal the instructions He would have you obey, and recommit to acting on your willingness to obey Him.

CHAPTER 7

"I WILL RICHLY REPAY WHAT YOU GIVE TO MY KINGDOM"

"Bring the whole tithe into the storehouse, that there may be food in my house. Test me in this," says the Lord Almighty, "and see if I will not throw open the flood-gates of heaven and pour out so much blessing that you will not have room enough for it."

—Malachi 3:10

God's economy is based upon biblical principles that He has outlined for us in His Word, and they include instructions in regard to fiscal management. God's economy is not based upon what is happening in our nation or around the world. God has given us promises in the Word of God, and as we practice His principles, we can securely stand on His promises. But we can't plead the promises of God if we aren't practicing His principles.

OBEDIENT GIVING

God outlines three steps of giving in the Bible. As we practice these principles of giving, we can count on God's promise to supply all of our needs, according to His riches in glory (see Phil. 4:19). The three ways we give back to God are through our firstfruits, our tithes, and our offerings.

Proverbs 3:9-10 says, *"Honor the LORD with your wealth, with the firstfruits of all your crops; then your barns will be filled to overflowing, and your vats will brim over with new wine."* As we honor the Lord with the firstfruits of our wealth, or our income, we will overflow with the blessings of the Lord. God doesn't want our "last fruits"; He wants our firstfruits as a sign that He comes first in our hearts. When we make the Lord our first love, rather than our money or our material possessions, He will take us to a place that we never could have reached on our own. He will put you in a car or a house that you could never afford in the natural. He will give you a promotion at work that exceeds your qualifications in the natural. God truly showers us with an overflow of blessings when He maintains the position of our "first love."

SUPERNATURAL BLESSINGS

I believe God not only wants the firstfruits of our income, but He wants the firstfruits of our day. We give Him the firstfruits of our day by spending time with Him in prayer and worship every morning. I also believe He wants the firstfruits of our week, which we give Him by keeping the Sabbath holy and consecrating ourselves and worshiping Him that day. When we give Him the firstfruits of our time, daily and weekly, then the remainder of our days and weeks are blessed. We supernaturally get more done than ever before. Things just fall into place. Supernaturally, all of our responsibilities are met in record time.

Malachi 3 tells us that we can "test" God in this principle of giving. When we tithe we can "test" God to be our Provider. It says He will throw open the windows of heaven. It doesn't say that He will just squeak open the windows of heaven in a stingy

manner, letting just a few blessings trickle out. It says He will *"throw open"* the *"floodgates"* of heaven and *"pour out so much blessing that you will not have room enough for it."* In other words, you will have more than enough. He is the God of more than enough. He will bless you with such an abundance that you will be glad to give it away to bless others!

I grew up on a farm, and Malachi 3:10 always reminds me of our tomato patch. Every time we planted tomatoes, we had so many that we would have to give them away. Yes, we used them for a part of our own provision (we sold them on our stand), but we always had so many that, in the end, we were giving them away like crazy. That's how it is with God. The more you sow into the kingdom of God, the more you have; the more you have, the more you sow. It's a beautiful cycle!

The Importance of Tithing

Again, we read in Malachi 3:10,

"Bring the whole tithe into the storehouse, that there may be food in my house. Test me in this," says the LORD Almighty, "and see if I will not throw open the floodgates of heaven and pour out so much blessing that you will not have room enough for it."

The word *tithe* actually means one-tenth. Don't think you can tithe 3 percent and have it covered. No, one-tenth is 10 percent. I have been shocked as I have heard Christians say, "Well, just start where you can. If you can only start at 3 percent, start there." I appreciate the fact that they were saying just start, but 3 percent of obedience is 7 percent short. God requires complete obedience. You can't afford *not* to give 10 percent of your income to the work of the Lord because of what's recorded in the verses just before Malachi 3:10.

Malachi 3:8-9 says,

Will a man rob God? Yet you rob me. But you ask, "How do we rob you?" In tithes and offerings. You are under a curse—the whole nation of you—because you are robbing me.

When we fail to tithe and when we fail to do the third step of giving—our offerings—we are under a financial curse because we are robbing God. You might say, "That's really strong." But that's what the Word of God says. I learned a long time ago that we shouldn't try to rewrite the Book. Don't try to ignore those Scriptures that you don't like and just focus on the ones you do. If you want to be blessed and prosperous, you must be careful to do *all* of the Word (see Josh. 1:8).

Give Like God—Extravagantly

God does not give sparingly. Romans 8:32 says, *"He who did not spare his own Son, but gave him up for us all—how will he not also, along with him, graciously give us all things?"* Even down to giving His own Son, God did not give sparingly, and neither should we. He set the ultimate example of generous giving, and we should strive to emulate Him in our giving through tithes, offerings, and alms.

Second Corinthians 9:6-7 says,

Remember this: Whoever sows sparingly will also reap sparingly, and whoever sows generously will also reap generously. Each man should give what he has decided in his heart to give, not reluctantly or under compulsion for God loves a cheerful giver.

God sowed His Son and reaped a family—you, me, and the rest of the Body of Christ. How much more generous could you give? And how much more blessed could you get? Verse 6 starts

with, *"Remember this...."* I believe God knew that we'd need the reminder. When times are tight financially, we need to remember to sow generously because we need to reap more generously than ever!

You Reap What You Sow

One day, during the most difficult financial season of my life, I was driving down our street when the Lord said to me, "Seed your need and know where to sow." He was revealing to me an important biblical principle that would enable me to successfully come through the battle I was in.

The principle I'm talking about is the law of sowing and reaping, which basically says that every seed produces fruit after its own kind. This principle is expressed more fully in Galatians 6:

> *Do not be deceived: God cannot be mocked. A man reaps what he sows. The one who sows to please his sinful nature, from that nature will reap destruction; the one who sows to please the Spirit, from the Spirit will reap eternal life. Let us not become weary in doing good, for at the proper time we will reap a harvest if we do not give up. Therefore, as we have opportunity, let us do good to all people, especially to those who belong to the family of believers* (Galatians 6:7-10).

This biblical principle established by the Lord works in the natural. Think about it: Tomato seeds produce tomatoes. Apple seeds produce apples. Orange seeds produce oranges. It also works in the spiritual realm. When we sow encouragement into the lives of others, we reap encouragement in our own lives. When we sow hope into others' lives, we reap hope in our own lives. When we sow financial seed into fertile "soil," such as churches and ministries that are aligned with God's purposes, we reap a financial harvest in our own lives. We reap whatever we sow. It doesn't say that we will reap "wherever" or "whenever" we sow, but that we will reap "*what*" we sow. So don't sow financial seed into a ministry and expect them to pay your bills. In return for blessing that ministry, God will send you your own blessing from a different source.

In this season of my life, the Lord taught me to get my eyes off of myself and what I was going through. He reminded me, "There's always someone hurting worse than you are. There's always someone who has been through more than you have. And there's always someone who has less than you." Talk about a convicting experience! So I started seeking out those individuals who were worse off than me and began sowing into their lives. Specifically, I looked for women who were in great need.

One night, the Lord prompted me to go to the prayer room at my home church. It was a lot later than I usually go out, but I went anyway because I knew the Lord was ordering my steps. I went to the prayer room, with Destiny beside me in her baby carrier, and started to pray. After a while, I got up to go to the restroom. It was then that I noticed another woman in the prayer room. She was sobbing uncontrollably. So I went over to her and began to minister to her. As it turned out, she was married to an abusive man, and he had just beaten her. I was blessed to be able to sow encouragement, hope, and love into her life.

This type of situation became a regular thing for me. The Lord would bring women across my path who needed me to sow into their lives, and as I did, I knew I was sowing my own need. It was amazing—as I encouraged them, I myself was encouraged. As I shared with them the hope we have in Christ, I too became filled with hope. God reminded me of something He'd told me during my early days of ministry: "Keep your eyes on Me and your heart on the needs of My people." Nothing had changed except my circumstances, and I couldn't allow my circumstances to cause me to get stuck in a focus on self.

As time passed, the Lord used me to minister to many women, which resulted in the healing of my own heart. One day, He revealed to me that there were single moms living just a few miles from our church who didn't know how they were going to feed their children dinner that night. I had spent years sitting in my "cushy" office at the church, completely oblivious to the fact that there were single moms in need nearby. There's nothing like first-hand experience to help you develop a heart of compassion for those in need. I didn't know how I was going to feed my own daughter, but I did know who my Provider was—the Lord God Almighty.

I started taking food—whatever I had in my pantry, really—to the single moms who lived in a housing project a few miles from the church. When I delivered the groceries, I would tell those moms about the love of Jesus—how He died on the cross for the forgiveness of their sins and rose again to conquer death and make it possible for them to spend eternity with Him. Every time I made a round of deliveries, I would come home to find a bag of groceries on my front porch! I was seeding my own need and reaping a miraculous harvest for Destiny and me, as well as for the kingdom of God. I came to understand fully Galatians 6:9: *"Let us not become weary in doing good, for at the proper time we will reap a harvest if we do not give up."*

Seed Your Need

When you yourself have a great need, that's a great time to sow! I don't believe in waiting until we have a need to sow, but keep sowing even during those difficult times. My family didn't wait until we were hungry before we sowed our tomato seeds. We looked ahead, knew we were going to need a harvest, and we sowed our seeds. And then, at harvest time, we had more than enough.

During times of great need, we must continue to sow. If you were hungry and the only thing you had was a pack of tomato seeds, what would you do? Would you eat the seeds, or would you plant them? Hopefully, you would be smart enough to plant them or sow them into good soil and expect a harvest to meet your need.

You can actually give your way to blessings! Proverbs 11:25 says, *"A generous man will prosper; he who refreshes others will himself be refreshed."* So the Word is telling us that the more we give, the more we will be blessed (as long as we are sowing on good soil). And as we refresh others by giving to them and blessing them, we ourselves will be refreshed and blessed. But a stingy person, on the other hand, has quite a different outcome. Proverbs 28:22 says, *"A stingy man is eager to get rich and is unaware that poverty awaits him."* God's economy is actually opposite of the world's economy. The kingdom of God is actually the upside-down kingdom, where you give to gain and you die to live! The world says hold on to everything you have so you can have it all. But in the kingdom of God, He says to give it all so you can have even more.

God has a special place in His heart for the poor, the fatherless, and the widows. As we reach out and bless them, we can't help but be blessed ourselves. Proverbs 19:17 says, *"He who is kind to the poor lends to the LORD, and he will reward him for what he has done."* God actually rewards and blesses those who give to the poor. As we give to the poor, the Word says that we are actually lending or giving to God. And whatever we do for one of the least of these, we do for the Lord (see Matt. 25:40).

One day, the Lord showed me Proverbs 28:27: *"He who gives to the poor will lack nothing, but he who closes his eyes to them receives many curses."* When I saw that Scripture, the Lord said to me, "Danette, you lack nothing because you have given to the poor." Wow! I was shocked! I had never known that Scripture, but I was living it out, and as a result, I was radically blessed.

It took a step of faith—a *big* step of faith—for me to get my eyes off of myself and to seek out others who had greater needs. Not only was my bank account hurting, but my heart was aching with the loss of a marriage and a dream. But when you do things God's way, everything else falls in place.

Reap the Rewards of Generous Sowing

Today I am totally debt-free, all because I obeyed God one step at a time with my giving. It came from giving to the poor, it came from my obedience to tithe and sow and give until I felt I couldn't give any more. Then God showed up—every day, every bill, every month! And what He did for me, He will do for you. Get your eyes off yourself, keep your eyes on Him, and obey every step of the way. This, too, shall pass. Just keep pressing your way—you are about to enter a new day!

One thing to keep in mind is that when we face temporary hardships in a godly way, responding in faith, God will get the glory when He brings us out of them. Make sure each season works for you and not against you. Making it work for you ensures that when you come out on the other side, your faith has been strengthened because you have learned to increase your dependence on God and to develop your prayer life. When you do those things, the people around you will see how much you trust God, and then, when you move out of that season, they'll know that He was the One who delivered you. God gets the glory when you mature through each season of life.

Little Keys to Abundant Provision

Key #7: Seed your need.

QUESTIONS FOR REFLECTION AND PERSONAL APPLICATION

1. It is a biblical principle that you reap what you sow. How have you seen this played out in your own life, whether in your finances or in another realm, such as your relationships, your career, or your times of intimacy spent with God?

2. An important lesson I learned from God was that I needed to "seed my need." What is one of the major needs you are facing right now? Can you think of a way to "seed" that need by giving to others? Give it a try and see how God works through you.

Prayer

Present to the Lord one of your needs, and ask Him to reveal how He would have you seed that need into the life of someone else. Thank Him for opening your eyes to see new ways to bless those around you.

CHAPTER 8

"You Can Trust Me to Guide You"

Trust in the LORD with all your heart and lean not on your own understanding; in all your ways acknowledge him, and he will make your paths straight.

—Proverbs 3:5-6

After my husband moved out, leaving me with an infant to raise and no income to rely on, I made a lot of assumptions based on my "wisdom" in the natural. I thought to myself, *Surely, the Lord wants me to move away from this area and all of its painful memories. Surely, the Lord wants me to secure a well-paying job.* My mother wanted me to move back home so that she could help me raise Destiny, and my initial reaction was, *Of course, that's what I should do. It makes sense.* Other appealing offers came in from various ministries asking me to join their staff.

Just days prior to an out-of-state trip to visit a ministry with which I was seriously considering taking a job, the Lord said to me, "Be careful where you pitch your tent." At the time, I had no idea what that meant. All I knew without a shadow of a doubt was that God had given me a warning I didn't fully understand until several months later.

After sending me that initial warning, the Lord began to speak to me through the example of Abraham. He said to me, "I'm the One who brought you to Virginia Beach. Don't let anyone or any circumstance get you out of My will." He was telling me not to let my circumstances dictate my future. His plans for me had not changed. I may have had no control over the choices my husband made, but I was responsible for all of the choices I had to make. The Lord made it clear that the place where I pitched my tent was critical to me, my daughter, and the call of God on my life.

The Lord spoke to me and showed me that the area to which I was thinking of moving would not be a good place to raise my daughter, especially without a father around. Years later, I discovered that this particular area was heavily populated with go-go bars and that pornography and other sexual perversions were rampant there. I also found out that the city and surrounding areas where we lived were among the top places in our nation to raise a family. God is so good! He knows everything, and He will reveal His perfect will to us if we take the time to seek Him.

WATCH WHERE YOU PITCH YOUR TENT

If we aren't careful where we pitch our tent, the results can be devastating. Our "tent" represents the place where we take up residence or even simply become familiar with. (In other words, it doesn't have to be a specific physical location or geographic area. It can even be a stock we invest in or a financial habit we adopt.)

In the twelfth chapter of Genesis, the Lord speaks to Abraham (when his name was still Abram) and tells him to leave his country and his people to go to a land that would eventually be revealed (see Gen. 12:1-3). The Lord explained to Abram what He

124

wanted to do through his life, and Abram responded in faith and obedience (see Gen. 12:4). As he traveled along, Abram sought the will of God for his every move. He cried out to God, asking Him where he ought to pitch his tent, and he added that he would built an altar there to memorialize his meeting with God—the place where he heard the voice of God and experienced His presence (see Gen. 12:6-8).

Meanwhile, Lot surveyed the land and chose for himself where to take up residence after parting from his uncle Abram. What he saw in the natural looked good; it must have been God's will, right? Wrong. But Lot never entertained the possibility of asking God about it. Instead, he *"chose for himself the whole plain of the Jordan and set out toward the east..."* (Gen. 13:11). Lot wasn't careful where he pitched his tent, and his entire family paid the consequences. He pitched his tent near Sodom, a city of great sin and wickedness (see Gen. 12:12-13). Since the people of Sodom were known to be sinful, Lot was flirting with disaster by choosing to live near them. It wasn't long before Lot was not only living near sin, but living in sin: An enemy people group *"also carried off Abram's nephew Lot and his possessions, since he was living in Sodom"* (Gen. 14:12).

If we pitch our tent outside of God's will, there's a costly price to pay. We can lose everything—all of our possessions, our children, our salvation, and even our lives. Yes, God loves us and will forgive us for our poor decisions, but it's better if we make the right choice at the outset. If you are at a crossroads, pray to the Lord and wait for His direction before moving forward. If you recently pitched your tent in a place where you now know is not God's will, be encouraged—a tent is, by definition, a temporary sort of dwelling place. You can repent, pull up those stakes, and move on. Don't waste time condemning yourself for past mistakes. Rather, repent and relocate into the will of God.

LET GOD LEAD THE WAY

Genesis 12:5 says that Abram

took his wife Sarai, his nephew Lot, all the possessions they had accumulated and the people they had acquired in Haran, and they set out for the land of Canaan, and they arrived there.

Many people set out to do God's will in their lives, yet they never "arrive there." The Word tells us that Abram *"set out for the land of Canaan, and...arrived there."* What accounted for Abram's success? First of all, he responded in faith and obedience to the Lord, even though he had no clue where He was leading him or why. Second, he sought the Lord concerning his every move. He didn't just listen to one part of the instructions and then assume he knew everything he needed to know. If we aren't careful, we can assume that we know all of the instructions regarding what we're supposed to do and how. When we make assumptions and act on them, we usually get into a big mess, only to wake up and wonder why we never reached our destination in God.

We must earnestly seek the will of God for every decision and then act in obedience, even if He tells us to do something we don't quite understand or don't like. Sometimes, it may take awhile to hear a clear word from God. Be patient as you await His directions, because His timing is perfect. Never presume to know His will for your life. Just as a severe rainstorm blocks our ability to see clearly in the natural, the emotional and financial storms of life obstruct our vision and make it all the more dangerous to act in our own knowledge and understanding. That's why it's crucial to wait on the Lord. *"I wait for the LORD, my soul waits, and in his word I put my hope"* (Ps. 130:5).

PITCH YOUR TENT WHERE GOD TELLS YOU TO

I can remember a time many years ago when I needed new office space for our growing ministry. I saw a location that I

thought would be perfect. My assistant and I went and laid hands on the front window and prayed as we "claimed" the office space for Joy Ministries. Well, we never got that particular office space. God did give us new office space—and it was much better than the space I had previously deemed "perfect for us." I'm so glad that God isn't in our control. He is in control, and He always sets us up to receive His best. I've also learned along the way that God doesn't need my help; He just needs my obedience. Abraham and Sarah tried to help God out, and they ended up with an Ishmael. God's best is always worth waiting for—always! Be patient, because your Isaac is on the way—and it's probably far better than anything you could have envisioned.

The wisdom of God is a stabilizing force. *"By wisdom a house is built, and through understanding it is established"* (Prov. 24:3). How do we receive wisdom? Like Solomon, we merely need to ask the Lord—He is extremely generous with His wisdom. *"If any of you lacks wisdom, he should ask God, who gives generously to all without finding fault, and it will be given to him"* (James 1:5). We never need to be bashful about asking God for wisdom because He bestows it without finding fault. He'll never roll His eyes and say, "Gosh, here comes Danette again, bugging Me for more wisdom."

Hebrews 11:6 says that God *"is a rewarder of those who diligently seek Him"* (NKJV). As we dwell in the presence of the Lord, He imparts His wisdom to us. We simply need to ask. Acknowledge Him as the Source of wisdom, as the psalmist did: *"How many are your works, O LORD! In wisdom you made them all..."* (Ps. 104:24). But there is a caveat: We must believe and not doubt. After exhorting us to ask God for wisdom, James went on to say,

> But when he asks, he must believe and not doubt, because he who doubts is like a wave of the sea, blown and tossed by the wind. That man should not think he will receive anything from the Lord; he is a double-minded man, unstable in all he does (James 1:6-8).

127

One valuable lesson I have learned is to trust my God-given discernment, which I developed during my time spent with the Lord. When we are close to Him, we can hear His voice and discern His leading. Then, when we leave the secret place and participate in daily life (never ceasing to abide in Him, of course), we won't be easily tempted to doubt what He has spoken.

I can remember the first time I received a word of knowledge from God. I was in church, praying at the altar, and by the time I had gotten up and returned to my pew, doubts had already begun to creep into my mind. The Lord spoke to me and revealed that the enemy had come in to steal the Word away from me. (See the Parable of the Sower in Luke 8.) If we begin to doubt, we become double-minded, since our mind is entertaining at the same time belief and unbelief. Pretty soon, this double-mindedness affects other areas of our lives, until we become *"unstable in all"* we do.

However, when we dwell in the secret place, we can remain stable and fixed under the shadow of the Almighty. *Fixed* is defined as "not readily movable; firmly implanted." When the enemy sees that you are not readily movable, he'll move on in search of somebody else to mess with. Don't live your life with what I call "meltdown mania." Live in the secret place, in the shelter of the Almighty, and declare, "My life is a meltdown-free zone!"

LET GOD GUIDE YOU THROUGH THE STORM

The apostle Paul had at least one thing in common with all of us—he experienced a significant number of storms in his life. Acts 27 recounts a literal storm he experienced on a ship en route to Italy.

> *…Sailing had already become dangerous because by now it was after the Fast. So Paul warned them, "Men, I can see that our voyage is going to be disastrous and bring great loss to ship and cargo, and to our own lives also." But the centurion, instead of*

listening to what Paul said, followed the advice of the pilot and of the owner of the ship (Acts 27:9-11).

Paul had heard from God, and he tried to tell those around him who were responsible for steering the ship. Unfortunately, they didn't listen to Paul. They listened to the experts. Sometimes you know something in your spirit that you try to communicate to others around you. Unless they have an ear to discern the Spirit of the Lord, they won't hear the same voice and may dismiss your input.

I recently had lunch with a couple, and the wife shared a story from their early years of ministry. They had completed their responsibilities in the city where they had been ministering and were seeking the Lord's will regarding their next assignment when an opportunity presented itself. It seemed too good to pass up, but the wife did not feel a sense of peace about it, and she told her husband. He responded, "I'm the decision-maker," and proceeded to move his family across the country. It ended up being a disaster. It wasn't long before they moved back to their original city and started fresh, seeking God anew for His direction.

Many of us have been through a similar experience at least once, whether we were trying to decide where to take a job, where to attend college, or even where to vacation. In Paul's situation onboard the ship, those who were in charge of making decisions chose to heed the experts' opinions instead of the wisdom of God. It is never wise to value "expert opinion" above God's opinion, which is based on His omniscience and always outweighs human knowledge. Listening to the experts can get you into deep trouble, especially when those experts rely on their own understanding instead of praying to the One in whom understanding begins. *"Great is our Lord and mighty in power; his understanding has no limit"* (Ps. 147:5). He shares His understanding with us, but we must open our ears and our minds to receive it.

Sure enough, *"Before very long, a wind of hurricane force, called the 'northeaster,' swept down from the island"* (Acts 27:14). When we ignore the voice of God, it doesn't take long for a storm to brew. In the case of Paul's shipmates, many of them were convinced that this storm would be the end of them.

> *After the men had gone a long time without food, Paul stood up before them and said: "Men, you should have taken my advice not to sail from Crete; then you would have spared yourselves this damage and loss. But now I urge you to keep up your courage, because not one of you will be lost; only the ship will be destroyed. Last night an angel of the God whose I am and whom I serve stood beside me and said, 'Do not be afraid, Paul. You must stand trial before Caesar; and God has graciously given you the lives of all who sail with you.' So keep up your courage, men, for I have faith in God that it will happen just as he told me"* (Acts 27:21-25).

God always comes to speak hope into our lives. He always comes to encourage us to press on through the storms. Through an angel, God had told Paul prophetically what was about to happen—the ship would be destroyed, but the passengers and crew would be kept safe. Do you know why the devil hates the prophetic voice of God? Because it always comes to encourage us and bring us hope. Satan is the exact opposite—he wants to overwhelm us with discouragement and feelings of hopelessness. But he is a liar! The truth is, even if your "ship" or something else is destroyed by the storm, you can trust God to bring you out unharmed.

Maybe you have lost your house, your car, your high credit score, or something else. Be encouraged—you aren't going to lose your life! Maybe the storm of bills is raging all around you, and you feel as if you will drown in debt. Hang on! You may lose some things, but the most important things will remain intact—you

and your relationship with God. Together, the two of you are the majority, and the battle isn't over until you emerge victorious.

Delayed but Not Derailed

Maybe you, like Paul, have been delayed on your way to your God-given appointment. Don't worry—despite temporary delays, you still have a destiny in God. Remember that *"what is seen is temporary, but what is unseen is eternal"* (2 Cor. 4:18). Your current season is just one stepping stone in a sequence of seasons leading to your eternal destiny.

Maybe your delay is due to you heeding the advice of experts. Perhaps a financial adviser led you down a destructive path or a stockbroker made some unsound suggestions. Maybe the "ship" of your finances is being tossed about on a sea of uncertainty, and you fear you'll sink any minute. Look to God, and He will calm the waters in due time.

Little Keys to Abundant Provision

Key #8: Watch where you pitch your tent.

Questions for Reflection and Personal Application

1. Have you ever jumped to a "logical" conclusion about how to proceed in a certain situation, only to be redirected by the Lord? What was the outcome?

2. How often do you consult the will of God before moving forward?

Prayer

Thank God for His all-wise guidance and for the privilege of being able to seek His will in every situation. Then ask Him for wisdom so that you might better discern His guidance in future situations.

CHAPTER 9

"SEEK ME, AND I'LL SPEAK TO YOU"

*You will seek me and find me when you seek me with
all your heart.*

—Jeremiah 29:13

Everywhere I go, people ask me, "How do you hear God's
voice? I want to hear His voice like you do." I always respond by
telling them, "Hearing God's voice is easy; it's obeying His voice
that's the hard part." Hearing His voice has a lot to do with our
position—again, it's crucial to sit at His feet and spend time praying, worshiping, and reading His Word. God is always speaking,
and He wants to speak to you even more than you want to hear
from Him. Position yourself daily to hear His voice. And then,
when He speaks, make sure to obey, even if you aren't thrilled
about His instructions.

A deliberate refusal to obey causes the voice of God to grow
faint. Before long, we'll hardly hear Him at all. Think about it: if
you were speaking to someone who ignored you, would you keep

on talking? More than likely, you would move on to someone else who was willing to listen to you.

DEVELOP A LIFESTYLE OF PRAYER

To hear from God, it's crucial to dwell in the secret place and develop a lifestyle of prayer. When we are in the presence of the Lord (our times of prayer, worship, and study of the Word), the Holy Spirit transforms us and gives us guidance. From our conception, God formed us in His very image (see Ps. 22:9-10; Gen. 1:26). Throughout our lives, the Holy Spirit transforms us more and more into the likeness of God's Son, Jesus Christ (see Rom. 8:29). Often, we need realignment!

I'm reminded of a time when the Holy Spirit gave me a realignment in my prayer life. Afterward, I felt totally transformed. As a minister, I'm required to hear from the Lord on a regular basis concerning what God wants to say to His people—my ministry partners who read my weekly newsletter, the viewers who watch my television show, or the people who attend the church services where I speak on Sundays. Not only that, but I need to hear from the Lord regarding every administrative decision I make in our ministry office. The Father's wisdom is indispensable to me as I manage our staff and mediate various issues. And I didn't even mention the wisdom I need in order to deal with my teenage daughter! Basically, I need to hear from God 24/7. That's a lot of hearing! But the details count.

God is a God of detail. If you could ask Noah, who built the ark, I'm sure he would agree! (See Genesis 6–7.) Seeking the details of God's will and then carrying them out in obedience are two vital steps in our quest to bear fruit in the kingdom of God.

I can hear from God; however, I can't just spend all my time hearing from the Lord for everyone else. I need to spend time with Him, one-on-one. I need to hear what He wants to say to me,

134

first and foremost. I need to keep my heart right and pure before the Lord. I need to keep my life on track with His will, and that is possible only when I schedule regular times of intimate prayer and fellowship with Him. That's the only way I can maintain the "garden" of my heart. I can't allow "weeds" to grow there. Just as weeds in a natural garden are plants that don't belong there, weeds in the heart are out-of-place emotions, such as fear, anger, bitterness, resentment, and envy. They're like the *little foxes that spoil the vines"* (Song of Sol. 2:15 NKJV). The vineyard of our heart bears fruit only as we keep it pure and weeded.

I can't just spend time in the outer courts, or the Holy Place. I must spend time regularly in the Holy of Holies. People are transformed in the Holy of Holies. Many people go to church all of their lives, yet they are never completely transformed; they are still bound by shackles that keep them from entering the Holy of Holies and finding total freedom in Christ.

Until the Lord realigned my prayer life, I had been spending time with Him daily in prayer, yet I hadn't taken the time to get to the Holy of Holies. It takes time and patience to get to the Holy of Holies. During this season of my life, I was very busy in ministry. I would go to bed exhausted and get up early enough the next morning to spend an hour or a half hour with the Lord. But I never gave myself enough time to press through to the Holy of Holies before starting my day. After three months of this, the Lord stopped me in my tracks and told me it was time for a realignment.

God knows our hearts even better than we know them ourselves, and He is faithful to realign us whenever necessary. I always say that if you stay in the Lord's presence until He is finished and He has released you, the next time you come before Him in prayer, you will pick up where He left off. If you leave before the Lord is done, next time, it's like starting all over again—pressing through, reaching for that place in His presence. I'm convinced that many people miss out on their healing or their deliverance because they never get close enough to the Lord to touch Him. The Word says that all who touched Jesus were healed (see Matt. 14:36; Mark 6:56). To touch someone, you need to get close enough, and that takes time.

Have you been taking the time to get close enough to the Lord to touch Him? Or have you been rushing around, cramming too many things into your day and keeping your time spent in God's presence on the "back burner" of your life? Don't put God on the back burner—put Him up front, and let Him crank up the fire of His Holy Spirit in your life. You will be glad you did!

ALLOW GOD TO PLOW THE GROUND OF YOUR HEART

In college, I was part of a group of young people who traveled across the nation on evangelistic trips. I was the treasurer, and I admired the president, who was an anointed preacher. One day, we were told that he was no longer the president because he had been involved in sin. As a young Christian, I was confused. *How can that be?* I wondered. *He preaches with such anointing, even though he has sin in his life!* As I grew as a Christian, I learned that the presence of God's anointing is no guarantee that an individual is right with Him.

That realization has remained at the back of my mind ever since, and now, as a minister myself, I make sure to keep my heart pure and my life right. So I spend time every day in the presence of the Lord through prayer, worship, and the study of His Word. It's in those times that the Lord deals with me and shows me the "little attitudes" that threaten to spoil the vine of my life, just like the "little foxes" in Song of Solomon 2:15. As we deal with the "little foxes" in our lives—the little offenses, the little lies, the little ungodly attitudes—we keep the "vineyards" of our hearts

pure and clean. That way, our anointing is true, and we are able to produce great fruit for God's kingdom purposes.

If I don't seek the Lord's pruning daily, my heart might fill with little foxes that aren't pleasing to the Lord, and it doesn't take long for little foxes to grow into big foxes. Allow the Lord to kick the little foxes out of the garden of your heart, and you won't have to worry about big foxes trampling your vines and thwarting your potential.

How far we go in God is really up to us. It's our choice. So, let's *"seek the LORD while he may be found; call on him while he is near"* (Isa. 55:6). Sometimes we won't experience immediate breakthrough when we pray. Sometimes we have to "plow the ground" in prayer, pressing our way persistently into His presence. We can't afford to give up! Faithful communication with God requires discipline, but it's worth more than anything.

How long should you pray? I always say that you should pray until the Lord is finished. Too often, we become tired or distracted, and we stop praying before the Lord is done. We look at our watch and think, *I guess God isn't going to give me an answer. I might as well get started on my to-do list for the day.* When we stop praying before God is finished with us, it will set us back the next time we pray, and we'll have to retrace our steps and re-plow the same ground in prayer. But when we stay in His presence until He is finished, we're able to pick up where we left off the next time we go to pray, and we enter into the awesome realm of His presence right away. It no longer feels like work. There we are, immediately in the presence of our Father.

Press Your Way into Prayer

If you pray out of a sense of duty or obligation, it won't be any fun, nor will it produce fruit in your life. Prayer should come from a passion for the Lord! It's fantastic and fun, if you do it the right way.

I have noticed that many people "push" their way through life instead of "pressing" their way. When you push your way into the job promotion so you can make more money, you may think that you're about to arrive, but before you know it, you've pushed yourself off of a cliff. When you push doors open, whether it's in your ministry, your business, or another realm, it's often the case that you're entering a level you aren't ready for just yet. When you push your way into a relationship, you are likely to end up disappointed, heartbroken, and emotionally distraught. But when you press your way into something, you move gracefully and with poise. Pressing is never impatient. When you press into the presence of the Lord through prayer, you can count on receiving clear marching orders from Him. You can have confidence that He will speak to you in that still, small voice and that you will know exactly what you are supposed to do.

When you push your way and purchase something you can't really afford, you can end up in debt over your head. When you push your way and buy something you really don't need, you can push yourself right into a corner where you really don't want to be.

Psalm 127:1 says, *"Unless the LORD builds the house, its builders labor in vain. Unless the LORD watches over the city, the watchmen stand guard in vain."* When you push your way, you are trying to "build the house" yourself—and it's only a matter of time before the walls come crashing down all around you.

MAINTAIN REGULAR FELLOWSHIP WITH THE DIVINE GARDENER

It's one thing to start right in our relationship with the Lord, but it's another thing to finish right. Many are called, but few are

138

chosen (see Matt. 20:16; 22:14 NKJV). The "chosen few" are those who maintain the garden of their hearts through regular times of intimate fellowship with God. He is the ultimate Gardener, and when we dwell in His presence, He has complete access to our hearts. He can prune them, taking away the dead or damaged parts and leaving only those plants that produce godly fruit. *"He cuts off every branch in me that bears no fruit, while every branch that does bear fruit he prunes so that it will be even more fruitful"* (John 15:2).

Tired of the botanical imagery? Maybe you would rather view life as a boxing game than a garden. That's how the apostle Paul liked to look at it. He wrote, *"I beat my body and make it my slave so that after I have preached to others, I myself will not be disqualified for the prize"* (1 Cor. 9:27). In other words, he needed to discipline his own flesh—severely—so that he would not become disqualified. What good is it if we are leading everyone else to the prize of salvation and eternal life with Christ and we ourselves become disqualified? Get in the ring with God, and you'll meet the qualifications to overcome Satan's schemes.

First Peter 5:8 says, *"Be self-controlled and alert. Your enemy the devil prowls around like a roaring lion looking for someone to devour."* The open door for him to devour individuals can come through an unkempt garden of the heart. But as a result of regular times of intimate prayer, we are able to resist him. We resist the open door of hard, unplowed ground in our hearts. The next verse says, *"Resist him, standing firm in the faith"* (1 Pet. 5:9).

When we submit ourselves to God and resist the enemy, he must flee: *"Submit yourselves, then, to God. Resist the devil, and he will flee from you"* (James 4:7). Submitting to the Lord involves walking in obedience to Him, and it's a practice that makes our hearts and lives Satan-proof. We then need to take things to the final step—resisting the devil. Through our continued obedience to the leading of the Holy Spirit and the truth of God's Word, we can resist his schemes. When the devil is unable to find an open door to our hearts, he will flee. So keep the door shut on the enemy and stay locked inside the safety of your prayer closet.

Time spent with the Lord saves our lives, physically and spiritually. Remember to obey Him; we need to know what it is that He expects from us. And we find that out by reading His Word and spending time in His presence daily. When you get close to the Lord through prayer, you don't care about anything else. Through prayer and fasting, we plow the soil of our hearts and make it ready for God to plant seeds that will yield an abundant harvest of peace and productivity in His kingdom. The vineyard of our hearts can be free from fear and other "little foxes," even in the area of our finances.

When you are really caught up in prayer, you lose track of time. But if you are caught up in time, you lose track of prayer. We should continually reach for a new level in our prayer lives. As we reach for that place, God grants us access. To *reach* is to stretch toward something. As we reach for a higher place in any area of life, it stretches us—our faith, our patience, our perseverance, and so forth. But if we expect to arrive at the desired level, we need to submit to the stretching process. Otherwise we'll never reach higher realms.

One key to reaching for a higher realm is seeing it first in your mind's eye. You'll never attain what you're reaching for if you don't know what it is! So set your sights on the destination to which God is calling you. Don't just feel your way there. Too many people just "feel" their way through life instead of reaching for what God has promised for them. A lot of them wait until they get up in the morning to see how they "feel" before planning their day. If we fail to plan, we plan to fail.

Pray in the Spirit

Ephesians 6:18 tells us to *"pray in the Spirit on all occasions with all kinds of prayers and requests. With this in mind, be alert*

and always keep on praying for all the saints." We need to pray *"in the Spirit,"* not with our natural minds. We should not pray out of our own will, but the will of the Father. As we pray in the Spirit, we can discern the heart and mind of God. Praying in the Spirit doesn't just mean praying in your prayer language. It means praying according to the leading of the Holy Spirit rather than formulating prayers by your natural thinking.

When we remain alert and *"keep on praying,"* we activate our Holy Spirit detector, which picks up on what the Lord wants us to know. We will be able to discern what the enemy is up to and know how to respond in order to thwart the schemes he has plotted against us.

Practical Steps to a Powerful Prayer Life

Wait on God

When we pray, we must learn to wait on God with patience and perseverance. So often, we just jump in and start spewing out everything that is on our hearts about every situation we can think of. But when we wait, we can pray powerful, fruitful prayers that line up with the will of the Father.

Keep a Detailed Record of What He Says

As I mentioned earlier, I keep a journal in which I try to write down everything God says to me. I would encourage you to do the same. The enemy comes immediately to steal the Word (see Matt. 13:19; Mark 4:15; Luke 8:12), so it's important for us to write it down. Even when God's voice is bold and loud, in a few days, you will probably have a hard time remembering some of the important details. When God speaks to you in a dream or a vision, write it down. You may not understand it completely; you may not even know if it was a dream from God. Even so, record it in detail before you forget it. Sometimes, the Lord opens the eyes of our understanding months or even years later.

Keep Pressing In

When we pray, we need to keep pressing in. We need to pray without time constraints. Now, I realize you can't spend endless hours every day in prayer, but you need to set aside blocks of time when you can wait on the Lord in prayer without any time constraints.

As you develop your prayer life, you should have a regular place and a regular time of prayer. Prayer and reading of God's Word should be your number one priority every day. As you have a set time and place in your daily routine, you will be more likely to maintain a regular prayer life. Also, it's important to set aside a certain location for prayer. My "prayer closets," up to this point in my life, have always been used for other things, as well. For instance, during the years when my daughter was young, my prayer closest was the bathroom floor. Today, my prayer closest is my living room floor. Someday, I hope to have a house that's large enough for me to be able to designate a prayer room for myself. In the meantime, my entire house is my prayer room, because my home is a haven of prayer.

Ephesians 6:13 instructs us, *"Therefore put on the full armor of God, so that when the day of evil comes, you may be able to stand your ground, and after you have done everything, to stand."* Our ability to stand depends largely on our prayer life. When you maintain a powerful prayer life, you can stand your ground, no matter what kind of financial "weather" you're experiencing.

LITTLE KEYS TO ABUNDANT PROVISION

Key #9: Press your way into prayer.

QUESTIONS FOR REFLECTION AND PERSONAL APPLICATION

1. Evaluate your prayer life. How often do you spend time in the Lord's presence? And how open are you to having Him "plow the ground" of your heart? Seek to develop a more intimate walk with Him in the days ahead.

2. When petitioning God for something, do you tend to press or to push your way into prayer? What has been the result in terms of His responses to you?

3. Do you currently keep a journal in which you record the instructions you get from God? If so, how has that impacted your prayer life? If not, consider starting one today and seeing how it transforms your relationship with your heavenly Father.

Prayer

Enter into the presence of God and ask Him to plow the ground of your heart—to reveal any areas you need to surrender to Him for pruning so that you may bear more fruit for His kingdom. Be sure to write down any words you receive from Him.

CHAPTER 10

"Your Hope Is Sure When It's in Me"

The LORD is good to those whose hope is in him; to the one who seeks him.

—Lamentations 3:25

Put [your] hope in God, who richly provides us with everything for our enjoyment.

—1 Timothy 6:17

And hope does not disappoint us, because God has poured out his love into our hearts by the Holy Spirit, whom he has given us.

—Romans 5:5

Some people look at their seemingly hopeless situations and pitch their tent in a pit of hopelessness. I myself have struggled with this tendency. There were many times when the state of my finances indicated that I had no reason to hope. Many days, I wanted to give up hope and pitch my tent in a place of defeat, even as I was seeking to follow the Lord's leading. Yet God's will is always for us to pitch our tent on a plot of hope! I had to choose to hang on to the "rope of hope"—God's Word—which includes such encouraging examples as Abraham, who refused to camp out at a place of despair.

Romans 4:18-21 records his legacy of believing God, in spite of what his circumstances seemed to indicate:

Against all hope, Abraham in hope believed and so became the father of many nations, just as it had been said to him, "So shall your offspring be." Without weakening in his faith, he faced the fact that his body was as good as dead—since he was about a hundred years old—and that Sarah's womb was also dead. Yet he did not waver through unbelief regarding the promise of God, but was strengthened in his faith and gave glory to God being fully persuaded that God had power to do what he had promised.

Against all hope in the natural realm, Abraham believed God and, through supernatural hope, saw the fulfillment of the promises God had made to him. He never would have become all that the Lord had told him he would be if he had chosen to pitch his tent in a place of hopelessness.

Maybe your circumstances seem hopeless right now. Well, your hope is not in the natural realm, right? The facts exist in the natural realm, but the truth exists in the supernatural realm. The truth—God's Word and what He says about things—always outweighs the facts. The facts didn't cause Abraham to weaken in his faith. He faced the facts; he didn't deny them. Yet, he did not waver through unbelief. He was actually strengthened in his faith because he was fully persuaded—not partially persuaded—that God had the power to do what He had promised. Have hope, and don't let the facts rule your life! The facts don't have any power over you. Put your hope in the truth—the Word of God—and it will never let you down.

Abraham knew God had the power to fulfill His promises, and so he hung on to hope in the supernatural realm. *"Let us hold unswervingly to the hope we profess, for he who promised is faithful"* (Heb. 10:23).

HOPE IN THE FACE OF HOPELESSNESS

God will bring us through every financial season if we hang on to the hope we have in Him. When Destiny was very young, her father—my ex-husband—died. As we were dealing with all of the painful emotions surrounding his death, I received a notice that Destiny's health insurance would automatically be cancelled at the end of the month because she had been on her father's policy. I also found out that I would no longer receive child support. After reviewing our divorce papers, I made a phone call to his former employer, only to find out that Destiny had not, in fact, been named the beneficiary on her father's policy. He did some research to see if she qualified for any other benefits, but when we spoke again, he said to me, "We've never had anyone fall through every crack like you, Ms. Crawford. I'm sorry." He regretfully informed me that Destiny's father had opted not to participate in the social security benefits offered by his employer. Yet the man encouraged me to contact social security, anyway. I followed his advice and found out about a small amount of money that my former husband had paid in when he was younger. The social security employee said, "Lady, we can't pay out what was never paid in."

Despite these discouraging circumstances, God was still in control. Even though we had fallen through every crack, the Lord had our back. He was simply setting us up to be totally dependent on Him. At the end of the month, I received a phone call from someone who asked what we needed. I quickly responded, "I need health insurance for Destiny. Her policy will be cancelled within days." The caller said, "Don't worry; we'll pay for her insurance." I hung up the phone feeling very relieved.

The next day, the phone rang again. It was the same person, this time calling with a different question: "How much do you owe on your home?" I responded with the amount, down to the penny, and heard this in response: "I'll tell you what. We're not going to pay for Destiny's insurance"—my jaw dropped—"but we are going to pay off your house for you." My smile was bigger than ever before. God is so good! At the time of my greatest need—I had $7.80 in my bank account—God brought my greatest blessing. When I received the cashier's check for the mortgage, I deposited it immediately and wrote a check to the mortgage company. My balance was back to $7.80, but my house had been paid off. Glory to God! Because our hope was not in our bank account, but in God, we received miraculous provision. If we keep our eyes on God, our faith has the power to change the facts.

DON'T LOSE HOPE

Sometimes, it's hard to believe that you can hope again, especially when you have been let down more times than you can count. The Bible says that *"hope deferred makes the heart sick, but when the desire is fulfilled, it is a tree of life"* (Prov. 13:12 AMP). *Hope* means "to look forward to with desire and reasonable confidence." When you hope, you expect with reasonable confidence that your desires will come to pass. *Defer* is defined as "to put off to a future time… delay." Hope deferred is a true test of faith and perseverance. Our hope may be deferred for a time, due to a number of possible reasons—circumstances beyond our control, the enemy's schemes, our own decisions, and so forth—but, when it is fulfilled, our joy will be that much greater. So guard your hope! In hope there is power to do great things for God. In hope there is power to see the promises of God fulfilled in our lives.

KEEP YOUR HOPES UP

Several years ago, I was ministering to a lady with cancer. As I was praying for her, the Lord revealed some things to me. At first, I was hesitant to tell her about them. I thought, *I don't want to get her hopes up.* The Lord immediately corrected me and showed me that faith and hope are closely connected and that "getting our hopes up" is what He wants to do. When our hope is up, our faith goes up, too. After all, faith is the substance of things hoped for (see Heb. 11:1 NKJV). The devil doesn't want you to get your hopes up, but God never wants you to let your hopes go down.

If your hope has been deferred and your heart is sick today, don't give up—*"**when** the desire is fulfilled, it is a tree of life."* The Scripture doesn't say *"if* the desire is fulfilled"; it says *"when"!* You can be confident that your desires will be fulfilled; the only unknown is when. We have this promise in Psalm 37:4: *"Delight yourself in the LORD and he will give you the desires of your heart."* As we delight in Him, if our desires don't line up with His will—which is His best for us—He lovingly begins to change the desires of our hearts. After all, even the heart of the king is in the hand of the Lord (see Prov. 21:1), and so are our hearts. God will change our desires, if need be, so that He may give us the desires of our hearts.

FOCUS ON PAST PROMISES FULFILLED

When my husband left me, I fasted and prayed as I stood in faith for his deliverance. When my hope was repeatedly deferred, my heart was sick; it was a very difficult time for me. The Lord taught me to focus on all of my longings that had already been fulfilled. For years, I had wanted a little girl with long blonde hair and big blue eyes. Well that longing had been fulfilled, so that is where I chose to set my focus.

If you are feeling heartsick due to deferred hope, start focusing on all the blessings you do have. Focus on all the desires that have been fulfilled in your life. We don't always understand why things turn out the way they do, but we know that we can trust in the Lord.

FUEL YOUR ENDURANCE WITH HOPE

Hope keeps you going, even when everything indicates that you're doomed for defeat. While others quit in the financial pits, you will endure to the very end and see the hand of God move on your behalf. We need to build a strong foundation of hope, which is the foundation of endurance, so that we will be able to endure every difficult season of life.

Hebrews 10:36 says,

For you have need of steadfast patience and endurance, so that you may perform and fully accomplish the will of God, and thus receive and carry away [and enjoy to the full] what is promised (AMP).

When I was studying the Word one day, this Scripture jumped off the page and hit me right between the eyes. As I read this verse, the Lord emphasized the phrase "you have need of steadfast patience and endurance." He got His point across, loud and clear. I had a need for patience and endurance. Patience has never been a prominent fruit on the vine of my life. I'm a mover and shaker—a visionary who, at any given time, has several goals I'm striving to accomplish for the Lord and His kingdom. That's great, except that I'm often impatient to see their fulfillment. I have places to go, people to see, and things to do, and my attitude is often, "Get out of my way or get run over." God wasted no time dealing with

150

that attitude! He told me that in order to fully accomplish His will for my life and enjoy the fullness of His promises to me, I needed patience. My immediate response was, "Lord, I don't have time for that." Case in point!

Patience is key for maintaining hope. Without patience, we're quick to quit, give up, or "help" God by rushing ahead with plans of our own. Hold on to hope and persevere to see the promises of God fulfilled in your life.

HOPE IN GOD, NO MATTER YOUR CIRCUMSTANCES

There is great power in hope. The enemy wants to make us feel hopeless, but God wants us to remain hopeful—brimming with hope! All of us will lose hope, from time to time, but we have a source of hope that never lets us down: the Lord God Almighty. When the psalmist was going through a period of despair, he said, *"Why are you downcast, O my soul? Why so disturbed within me? Put your hope in God, for I will yet praise him, my Savior and my God…"* (Ps. 42:5-6). When our hope is in God, we have no need to feel downcast or disturbed, because God is always faithful. As long as we are hoping in the right thing, we have boundless power and inexhaustible hope. I want to encourage you to watch your words and the words that others speak to you, which may be used by the enemy in an attempt to rob you of hope.

Later in the Psalms, we read, *"The LORD delights in those who fear him, who put their hope in his unfailing love"* (Ps. 147:11). God's love for us is unfailing. Maybe you feel hopeless today because you put your hope in something or someone other than the Lord. People can let us down. Circumstances can disappoint us. Plans can fall through. But God is ever faithful to fulfill His promises. When our hope is in the Lord, we can rejoice, regardless of our circumstances.

The apostle Paul wrote, *"May the God of hope fill you with all joy and peace as you trust in him, so that you may overflow with hope by the power of the Holy Spirit"* (Rom. 15:13). In other words, God wants to fill us with joy and peace, but we have to allow Him to do so. Our God—the God of hope—will fill us with His joy and peace *as* we trust in Him! We need to trust the people in our lives, but we shouldn't put our trust in them; we trust in the Lord alone. The day will come when others betray us, but we won't lose hope if we haven't been trusting in them. God wants you to overflow with hope by the power of His Spirit in your life. In other words, He wants you to be a river of hope that overflows to others around you on a daily basis.

When we are filled with joy and peace, we have the strength to withstand seasons of hardship. Nehemiah 8:10 says, *"...The joy of the LORD is your strength."* If the enemy can succeed at stealing our hope, he can steal our joy and thereby deplete our strength. The weaker we feel, the easier it is for the enemy to convince us to throw in the towel and give up. Remember, quitters never win, while those who never quit can never be defeated.

For some of you, it's time to dream again. When you go through loss, you have to continually guard your hope. Maybe you have lost a loved one through death or divorce, and you have also lost a sense of hope. Maybe you have lost your job, your home, or maybe your complete life savings. Let the God of hope comfort you today in a way that only He can. Make Him your hope, and you'll never feel hopeless again.

HOPE ENABLES YOU TO REJOICE IN
YOUR SUFFERINGS

...And we rejoice in the hope of the glory of God. Not only so, but we also rejoice in our sufferings, because we know that suffering produces perseverance; perseverance, character; and character, hope. And hope does not disappoint us, because God

has poured out his love into our hearts by the Holy Spirit, whom he has given us (Romans 5:2-5).

We don't rejoice *because of* our sufferings and difficult seasons, but we can—and we should—rejoice in the midst of our sufferings because we know the ultimate outcome: *"All things work together for good to those who love God, to those who are the called according to His purpose"* (Rom. 8:28 NKJV). Trials and tribulations don't have to steal our hope. In fact, in those times, our hope should increase because we know that a better season is just around the corner.

Isaiah 40:31 says that *"those who hope in the LORD will renew their strength. They will soar on wings like eagles; they will run and not grow weary, they will walk and not be faint."* When you hope in the Lord, you renew your strength because the God of hope fills you with joy and peace as you trust in Him. The joy of the Lord is your strength, so there you go! As you wait on the Lord, spending time in His presence as you worship Him, pray to Him, and study His Word—you are filled with hope and strength.

Then before you know it, you'll be soaring! *Soar* is defined as "to rise or aspire to a higher or more exalted level." Eagles soar into storms and rise above them. It's worth noting that eagles don't fly in flocks, like geese do; they soar alone. In some seasons, we may feel alone, but that's when we learn to soar! That's when we learn to rise above our circumstances in order to ascend to a higher level in our faith. When you soar on wings of true hope, you'll never grow weary or tired, even as you wait for the sun to shine again. We can soar high on wings as eagles, no matter what our bank account looks like.

HOPE BUILDS DETERMINATION
AND EXPECTATION

There is power in expectation—power to overcome challenging circumstances. Remember, hope is desire accompanied by expectation and anticipation. Your level of determination relates directly to your level of expectation. If your expectations are low and you assume you'll fail, your determination level will also be low, practically guaranteeing that your prediction will come true. However, if you have high expectations of success, you will be determined to succeed, no matter what!

You never birth anything you aren't first expecting. I was expecting my daughter for nine months before I gave birth to her. If you aren't expecting to make it through the storm, you won't have the determination to weather all the wind and rain.

There are two main elements that can increase your likelihood of being defeated by a storm: broken focus and discouragement. Distractions can cause you to lose focus. In the midst of every storm, stay focused on where you know your ship is headed, and don't entertain negative thoughts, which will discourage you and tempt you to abandon ship. If the enemy can discourage you, his job becomes easy; but when you stay encouraged, there's nothing that can stop you!

> *In an attempt to escape from the ship, the sailors let the lifeboat down into the sea, pretending they were going to lower some anchors from the bow. Then Paul said to the centurion and the soldiers, "Unless these men stay with the ship, you cannot be saved"* (Acts 27:30-31).

Paul told the crew that they needed to stay onboard and not give up. They couldn't abandon ship. Maybe today you are on the verge of bailing out. God is saying to you, "Don't abandon ship!" Just hang on. These delays weren't in your plans, but the Man with the plan—God—still has you in His hands! Don't let the storm get on the inside of you. Keep your expectations high and your determination up because you're about to make it to shore! Your finances are about to regain solid ground.

154

HOPE FOR THE FUTURE

Psalm 119:74 says, *"May those who fear you rejoice when they see me, for I have put my hope in your word."* Through prayer and study of God's Word, we renew our spirits and restore our hope. God's Word is truth, and the truth that we know will set us free (see John 8:32). As we read the Word, we come to know the truth, which frees us to hope. By grabbing hold of the rope of hope—God's Word—we restore our hope so that it carries through every financial season, no matter how challenging, and leads us to a bright future. The prophetic voice of God, or His *rhema* Word, always lines up with His written Word. The prophetic voice of God refreshes us, builds us up, and encourages us by restoring our hope.

In May 2001, Joy Ministries held its first annual Mother's Day Celebration, and we've been celebrating the event ever since. The purpose is to honor single moms, widows, and military wives whose husbands are deployed. Women come from all over the community, and we bus in others from subsidized housing neighborhoods, battered wives' shelters, assisted living facilities, and homeless shelters. Every mother in attendance, along with her children, enjoys a delicious meal, receives a Mother's Day gift, and attends a special program, during which I preach a word of hope and encouragement, outlining the plan of salvation and giving everyone an opportunity to accept Christ as Lord and Savior.

For several years, we gave each mother a framed Scripture verse—Jeremiah 29:11, which reads, *"For I know the plans I have for you,' declares the LORD, 'plans to prosper you and not to harm you, plans to give you hope and a future.'"* I received a leftover gift each year, and it was always a prophetic word for me. God kept saying the same thing over and over to me, and it was a great source of encouragement, refreshing and refilling my hope year after year. What a thrill to know that God was going to prosper me! At home, I was believing God to provide me with toilet paper and groceries; through my ministry, I was reaching out to other single moms in need. As a result, God was restoring my hope and assuring me of the great future He had for me. The prophetic voice of God refreshes and restores hope just when we need it the most.

Maybe you are losing hope in your future. Maybe your current financial season has you believing God for groceries and toilet paper. If that's the case, Jeremiah 29:11 is for you today. God knows His plans for you—plans to prosper you and to give you a future—and He wants you to spend time in His presence so that He can reveal those plans to you. There is a profound connection between your hope and your future. The enemy knows that if he can steal your hope, he can thwart your future. But you and God aren't going to let that happen!

God never gives up on anyone, and He hasn't given up on you, so don't give up on yourself! At a person's lowest point of losing hope, the lying spirit of suicide tries to creep in. Yes, suicide is a spirit; don't allow yourself to entertain it. Suicide is never the answer. Jesus Christ is the answer, for He alone brings hope and restoration. It may seem like there is no way out of the deep, dark pit of debt, but God always makes a way. He will bring you out if you hang on to the hope He's extending to you today. Remember, after every storm there's a beautiful new day. So hang on to hope—the storm clouds will be parting soon!

LITTLE KEYS TO ABUNDANT PROVISION

Key #10: Focus on past promises fulfilled.

QUESTIONS FOR REFLECTION AND PERSONAL APPLICATION

1. Have you ever been in a situation that seemed completely hopeless? How did you get through it? Considering the current state of your spiritual life, would you deal any differently with that type of situation today?

2. What would you consider to be the greatest source of hope in your life? How has that affected the way that you face trials and triumphs?

3. What did the apostle Paul mean when he said that he rejoiced in his suffering? Are you able to make the same statement?

Prayer

Praise God for the hope that you have in Him. Then pray that He would truly become your greatest source of hope so that you might say with the apostle Paul, "I rejoice even in the midst of suffering."

Chapter 11

"I've Got Great Plans for You"

"For I know the plans I have for you," declares the LORD, "plans to prosper you and not to harm you, plans to give you hope and a future."

—Jeremiah 29:11

We discussed the above Scripture verse at the end of the previous chapter, but it's such an important truth that we're going to explore it now in greater detail. God has great plans for you—hallelujah! And as a case in point, we're going to look at the life of Joseph and how it illustrates the process by which God positions someone according to His plans for his destiny.

Positioned According to His Plan

God positions us for our palace, or our destiny, and He then prepares us at His chosen place of positioning. In addition to being a place of preparation, God's place of positioning for you will also be a place of prosperity. Finally, that place of positioning will prove to be a place of promotion after you have been faithful to submit to the steps of God's positioning process. So God positions us, and then He prepares us in such a way that we prosper and eventually get promoted to our "palace," or our destiny in the Lord.

The positioning process is designed to do something *in* us so that, later, the Lord can do something *through* us. God positions us to prepare us, and then He prospers us in many different areas of our lives—financially, spiritually, emotionally, and so forth.

If you perceive the positioning process with natural eyes only, you are likely to get discouraged, and you may even give up. Often God's positioning process doesn't look anything like what we thought it would—or what we want it to look like. Part of God's positioning process for Joseph was the pit—a minor detail that was left out of the original vision God gave him concerning his destiny for the Lord! It's during those days of the positioning process that God prepares us by working on our hearts, our attitudes, and our faith and trust in Him.

You don't have to understand God's positioning process, but you do have to trust God. I have come to understand that I don't have to understand why God is telling me to do something or why He is requiring something of me. All I have to do is trust Him and obey. Remember, Proverbs 3:5-6 says, *"Trust in the LORD with all your heart, lean not unto your own understanding. In all your ways acknowledge him, and he will make your paths straight."* When we finally get to the point in our walk with God where we understand that *we don't understand*, God can really use us. We don't even have to be comfortable with what He is telling us to do. You know, your flesh doesn't have to be comfortable in order for you to be obedient!

Positioned is the place where you are located, especially in relation to other people, objects, or events. God positions us in relation to other people and things in a way that enables us to fulfill His purposes for our lives. God was strategically positioning

Joseph when his brothers threw him in the pit. Joseph had many opportunities to quit, to get a bad heart attitude, and to doubt the word God had given him. Yet Joseph kept his eyes on the vision and submitted to God's positioning process.

PROPHETIC INSIGHTS

When Joseph shared his God-given dream with his brothers, he wasn't expecting the reaction that he received. Genesis 37:6-7 says,

He said to them, "Listen to this dream I had: We were binding sheaves of grain out in the field when suddenly my sheaf rose and stood upright, while your sheaves gathered around mine and bowed down to it."

Wow! That's exciting. God had spoken prophetically to Joseph concerning his future, and Joseph knew that he would become a great leader. But he didn't know that he would have to go through a pit to get there. Even in Joseph's second dream, in which the sun, moon, and eleven stars bowed down to him (see Gen. 37:9), there was still no mention of a pit!

Looking back over my life, there have been many times when God spoke prophetically to me concerning things to come. Getting that prophetic word was exciting and encouraging because the voice of the Lord always builds up, edifies, encourages, corrects, and gives direction. We need more of His prophetic voice in our lives. God wants each of us to hear His prophetic voice on a regular basis. The devil hates the prophetic because it brings hope into the lives of God's people and works against his plan to steal, kill, and destroy (see John 10:10). But God's desire is to fill us with hope.

For nine years, I have held a Breakthrough Miracle Service in the Hampton Roads area of Virginia on the first Saturday of every month. The Lord brings the prophetic word to His people, and they leave blessed and encouraged. I just witnessed it again this month. God wants to give us that boost of encouragement and direction regularly so that we have the hope, the strength, and the confidence we need to pull through the difficult times on the way to the fulfillment of our God-given dreams and visions.

God had already spoken to Joseph about his ultimate destiny, and so, when Joseph found himself in the pit, he knew it was only temporary. No, God didn't allow Joseph to know *all* of the details or the fine print of the "road map" to his destiny, but He gave him what he needed—the final destination. I believe God sometimes does it that way so that we won't decline to take the trip before we even get started.

ALLOW GOD TO BIRTH YOUR DREAMS

We must have a dream before God ever positions us for the fulfillment of that dream. After conceiving the dream, we must believe it. First, we receive the dream—or vision—from the Lord, and then we must conceive it and believe it—and that takes faith. Then, and only then, God positions us in order to see the dream come to pass.

I strongly believe in having God-inspired goals, both short-term and long-term. Proverbs 29:18 says, *"Where there is no vision, the people perish..."* (KJV). Both Joseph and Abraham had God-inspired goals, and it was those goals that keep them pressing their way to the new day that the Lord had for them.

In order to fulfill God-inspired goals, we must first have them. Most people live day-to-day, week-to-week, year-to-year without any goals. You will never fulfill your goals if you don't have any—that's a no-brainer, right?

Second, your goals need to be inspired by God. Some people finally get goals, but their goals are just that—their goals! They aren't from the Lord. If you are going to be successful, you must have God-inspired goals. Remember, Psalm 127:1 says, *"Unless the LORD builds the house, its builders labor in vain. Unless the LORD watches over the city, the watchmen stand guard in vain."* If you are chasing after your own goals, you are laboring in vain trying to build your own house. But when you have God-inspired goals, you are hearing and cooperating with the voice of the Holy Spirit in how He wants you to obey His lead as He builds the house or the vision for your life.

Last, after you have God-inspired goals, you must desire to see them fulfilled more than anything. The people in Jerusalem wanted to rebuild the wall around their city, but they gave up after many unsuccessful attempts. Yes, they had a God-inspired goal, but they got discouraged and gave up. They just accepted things the way they were, and they learned to live with it—broken-down walls. They had a desired goal, but they never fulfilled it.

When you set out to fulfill your God-inspired goals, don't think for one minute that the devil is going to take it sitting down! He will try to discourage you, distract you, lie to you, buffet you— anything to prevent you from fulfilling those God-inspired goals. So don't be surprised when the attacks come. But be ready, stay encouraged, and never stop pressing toward the mark!

Nehemiah 6:15 says, *"So the wall was completed on the twenty-fifth of Elul, in fifty-two days."* The walls that laid in ruins for nearly a century and a half were rebuilt in record time! As Nehemiah pressed past opposition, as he focused on his God-inspired goal, he encouraged the people to work together, and the goal was completed in less than two months. It took unity and encouragement, but God worked through them. When we are focused on the goals the Father wants us to pursue, we will see the seemingly impossible manifest before our very eyes.

Keep Your Eyes on the Prize, Not the Pits

After receiving his life-changing dreams from the Lord, Joseph went through many surprising stages of the positioning process. First, he went to the pit, and then he was sold into slavery, and then he was thrown into prison, all for no fault of his own. It wasn't until after all of this that he finally reached the palace!

I knew for many, many years that I was called to hold crusades and city-wide outreaches and events in Latin American nations long before I started doing so. But when I finally got started, I experienced some "surprises" that had not been a part of my original vision. I will never forget Destiny's first mission trip. When she was only fifteen months old, she traveled to Bolivia with me. All of the stuff I thought would be challenging wasn't. I changed diapers on the plane without any problems; she didn't cry or fuss, even though our travel time totaled twenty-four hours each way. She really was the perfect angel as we traveled. But once we got to Bolivia, everything changed. I awoke one night to find hundreds of little bugs crawling on my baby. Now, let me explain one thing to you—I don't do bugs! Yes, I grew up in the country, and my dad tried really hard to make me into a country girl, but it never worked! And the bug deal didn't go over well with me, especially when they were crawling on my baby in the middle of the night. I was told, "They are only ants." But to me, a bug is a bug, and I don't do bugs!

There were other "surprises" that I will refrain from mentioning. My point is, I had to focus on what God had told me I was called to do there in Bolivia. The revealed dream or vision is what causes you to focus and hang on for the ride, pits and all!

Joseph soon learned that he would have to separate from his family in order to see the fulfillment of his dream. Genesis 37:10-11 says,

164

When he told his father as well as his brothers, his father
rebuked him, and said, "What is this dream you had? Will
your mother and I and your brothers actually come and bow
down to the ground before you?" His brothers were jealous of
him, but his father kept the matter in mind.

Sometimes, God's positioning process hurts. It can even separate us from the people we love. Joseph's own brothers were jealous
of him and hated him all the more when they found out about his
dreams. Yet God gave Joseph an even better relationship with his
family before it was all over.

GOD'S GREAT PLANS ALWAYS GET US OUT OF OUR COMFORT ZONES

God always requires us to get out of our comfort zones in order
to bring us into our potential zones. For many of you, God has
strategically placed you where you are. He has strategically orches-
trated circumstances and people around you. *"Consider it pure joy,*
my brothers, whenever you face trials of many kinds, because you
know that the testing of your faith develops perseverance" (James 1:2-
3). God has strategically positioned you for the palace, but there
are many stages of the positioning process. That's why it's crucial
to stay focused on the original vision, or what I call the "finish
line," all the way through each stage.

God is always in charge, even when it doesn't look like it.
Genesis 37:18 says, *"But they saw him in the distance, and before*
he reached them, they plotted to kill him." Sometimes other people
will notice that God is raising you up for a purpose and will plot
to "kill you," figuratively speaking, by thwarting your potential.
They may "kill you" with their words of negativity. Your dream or
vision may be threatening to them—it may make them feel intimidated and insecure, because they fail to realize that God wants to

do great things through them, too. Whatever the case, never let someone else's issue become your issue. You have enough of your own issues to deal with! Don't listen to anyone who speaks against you, because it's a reflection on that person's insecurities, not your qualities. When Joseph was in the pit, his brothers were still the ones with the problem. He wasn't worthy of their rejection. "...*Out of the overflow of the heart the mouth speaks*" (Matt. 12:34; see also Luke 6:45). So they were only reflecting their own hearts.

God is still in control, even when it looks as if someone else is holding the reins. Every single time the enemy tries to pull a fast one on you—even if he uses someone you love dearly—God will work for good what the enemy meant for evil. It never matters what people plot or plan; it only matters what God has planned, because His plans always come to pass. All we must do is stay on course and keep our hearts right.

Genesis 37:19-20 says,

"Here comes that dreamer!" they said to each other. "Come now, let's kill him and throw him into one of these cisterns and say that a ferocious animal devoured him. Then we'll see what comes of his dreams."

Always remember—it doesn't matter what they say; it only matters what God says. Don't focus on people or what people are saying or doing. Focus on God and God alone.

Genesis 37:21-22 says,

When Reuben heard this, he tried to rescue him from their hands. "Let's not take his life," he said. "Don't shed any blood. Throw him into this cistern here in the desert, but don't lay a hand on him."...

The truth is, Joseph's brothers could go only as far as God allowed them to. Joseph was being positioned for the palace; he wasn't going to lose his life. Even if the positioning process

166

kills your flesh, God won't let it kill you! There is nothing you will face along the way that God didn't allow. Again, even when Satan means for it to take you out, God will work it for your good. Remember, God uses the positioning process to prepare you.

God was preparing Joseph in his character and faith all along the way.

Now Israel loved Joseph more than any of his other sons, because he had been borne to him in his old age; and he made a richly ornamented robe for him. When his brothers saw that their father loved him more than any of them, they hated him and could not speak a kind word to him. Joseph had a dream, and when he told it to his brothers, they hated him all the more (Genesis 37:3-5).

FAVOR IS KEY TO PURPOSEFUL POSITIONING

While Joseph was hanging out in the pit, it didn't look like he was positioned to prosper. It actually looked like a dead end. In reality, it was a direct route to his palace. You can be in what looks like a dead end situation or position. Yet like Joseph, you can find favor everywhere you go when you are obedient to the Lord, because you know that He will position you to prosper in every area of your life.

UNWAVERING FAITH EARNS GOD'S FAVOR

Although Joseph was thrown into a pit and sold into slavery, he prospered because he never wavered in his faith in the Lord.

The LORD was with Joseph and he prospered, and he lived in the house of his Egyptian master. When his master saw that the LORD was with him and that the LORD gave him success in everything he did, Joseph found favor in his eyes and became his attendant. Potiphar put him in charge of his household, and he entrusted to his care everything he owned (Genesis 39:2-4).

Joseph prospered with success and favor. As Jesus was growing up, He *"grew in wisdom and stature, and in favor with God and men"* (Luke 2:52). I pray this Scripture over myself regularly, and I would encourage you to do the same. I say, "Lord, I thank You that, just like Jesus did, I grow in wisdom, in stature, and in favor with God and men today." This was not just for Jesus; it's also for you and me today. When you have the favor of God, you can't help but have the favor of people.

FAVOR MAY BRING OPPOSITION FROM OTHER PEOPLE

Sometimes other people *hate* to see you walk in favor. They fail to realize that God would extend the same favor to them for their purpose in God, and they chose to allow jealousy to control their hearts and their heart attitudes. Joseph's father symbolizes to us our heavenly Father. Joseph's father gave him a richly ornamented robe, and what his father gave him, no one could take away, as hard as they tried.

So when Joseph came to his brothers, they stripped him of his robe—the richly ornamented robe he was wearing—and they took him and threw him into the cistern. Now the cistern was empty; there was no water in it (Genesis 37:23-24).

Out of their jealousy, Joseph's brothers tried to take away what his father had given to him. I say "tried" because that's the key word. People can try to take away what the Lord has given you, including your call, but what God has ordained will remain! Although Joseph was stripped of his robe, God gave him more than double for his trouble—but it didn't happen overnight.

FAVOR GUARANTEES GOD WILL ORDER YOUR STEPS

There really are no coincidences in God! The very next verse goes on to tell us in Genesis 37:25 that

As they sat down to eat their meal, they looked up and saw a caravan of Ishmaelites coming from Gilead. Their camels were loaded with spices, balm and myrrh, and they were on their way to take them down to Egypt.

It "just so happened" that this caravan was passing right by them. It "just so happened" that they were going down to Egypt. None of this was a coincidence—God was ordering Joseph's steps! *"If the LORD delights in a man's way, he makes his steps firm; though he stumble, he will not fall, for the LORD upholds him with his hand"* (Ps. 37:23-24). Joseph was a man in whose "way" God delighted, and He was in control of his every step—including the steps that put him in the pit!

Psalm 90:17 says, *"May the favor of the Lord our God rest upon us; establish the work of our hands for us—yes, establish the work of our hands."* When you understand that the favor of God is what establishes the work of your hands, you stop trying to do things in your own strength. Remember, *"Unless the LORD builds the house, its builders labor in vain..."* (Ps. 127:1). Let God do the building!

As God's favor rests upon you, He establishes you and all that pertains to you. Favor begins with a right relationship with God. Proverbs 8:35 says, *"For whoever finds me* [wisdom] *finds life and receives favor from the LORD."* All favor begins with right relationship with the Lord. If you are trying to obtain favor any other way, you are doing it in your own strength.

Promotion always comes from the Lord. Favor is defined as approval, and when you have God's stamp of approval, that's all you need! There are four important keys to favor—where, when, what, and why. You open yourself up to the favor of God when you are where you are supposed to be, when you are supposed to be there, doing what you are supposed to be doing, and doing it for the right "why"—the proper heart motive. That's what happened to Esther. She had exceptional favor with the king because she was where she was supposed to be (the palace), when she was supposed to be there (during the search for a new queen), doing what she was supposed to be doing (following whatever the palace staff told her to do), all for the right heart motive (for the purpose of saving her people, the Jews). As a result, she made history!

You can't be at the right place at the wrong time and expect to have God's favor. Esther 2:17 says,

> *Now the king was attracted to Esther more than to any of the other women, and she won his favor and approval more than any of the other virgins. So he set a royal crown on her head and made her queen instead of Vashti.*

Esther's character of obedience attracted the king and won his favor. Similarly, our obedience attracts the King of kings and earns us His favor.

FAVOR YIELDS SUPERNATURAL FRUIT

God's favor upon your life can supernaturally get your bills paid and your needs met. Not too long ago, we were fund-raising for a certain outreach we had planned for the local community, and I felt a nudge in my spirit to go to a certain businessman in our community and ask him for a donation. He is not a Christian, to my knowledge, but he has a heart for helping disadvantaged, fatherless children, which is one of our main missions. As I walked in the door, he greeted me with a smile and said, "I was wondering when you were coming. I have a check waiting for you." I didn't even have to ask. Not two minutes after I entered his office, he was ready to hand me a $1,000 check. When an unsaved businessman has a sizeable check waiting for you, you know you have the favor

of God! I wasn't even going to ask for $1,000; I was going to ask for $500. O, me of little faith!

Matthew 7:7-8 says,

Ask and it will be given to you; seek and you will find; knock and the door will be opened to you. For everyone who asks receives; he who seeks finds; and to him who knocks, the door will be opened.

The favor of God is just waiting for you to do your part: ask, seek, and knock. When you have the favor of God, it follows you through every season of life, financial and otherwise.

That financial miracle, that raise, that bill you need to be reduced may all just be waiting for you to ask. Years ago, when I was working on staff at a large church, I had an annual review, and I was anticipating a pay increase of several thousand dollars. Yet when the person conducting my review asked me how much of an increase I was expecting, I was moved by the Holy Spirit to respond, "How much of an increase do *you* think I should receive?" I'm glad I didn't specify an amount, because he had a number in mind that was about five times as much as I had been hoping for. The Lord knew that I was about to ask for an amount that was too small, and because His favor was upon me, He made sure I didn't say something that might have earned me a smaller pay raise.

God Provides at His Place of Positioning

Each of us needs divine provision for the vision God has given us, and we can expect to receive it at God's chosen place of positioning. There were many times when I wanted to move away from the Virginia Beach area, especially after my husband left. But the Lord made it clear that He wanted me to stay there, and as I kept doing what He had called me to do, I received a constant supply of His provision.

171

Remember, Isaiah 1:19 says, *"If you are willing and obedient, you will eat the best from the land."* The key word is *if.* Our success depends upon our choices. *If* we are willing and obedient, we will step into God's best for us. It's easy to be willing, but harder to be obedient. Many times I've prayed, "Lord, help me to be willing to be obedient." Even Jesus acknowledged that *"The spirit indeed is willing, but the flesh is weak"* (Matt. 26:41 NKJV; Mark 14:38 NKJV). In other words, we have to carry our willingness all the way through to obedience. If we bring our flesh into submission to our spirit and walk obediently along the path God has laid out for us, we set ourselves up to receive God's blessings, because obedience always brings blessings.

God wants to position you and me to prosper spiritually, emotionally, physically, and financially. As we submit to the positioning process of the Holy Spirit, we will step into our Father's abundant provision. In other words, we have to be where we are supposed to be, when we are supposed to be there, doing what we are supposed to be doing—and for the right reasons—to receive the provision we need.

If the Lord tells you to take a job that pays half of what you're making right now, you had better obey. If He prompts you to move elsewhere, but you decide you'd rather stay put, don't expect any blessings. The key is to obey out of a belief that God will bless us. As we submit to the will of the Father and allow ourselves to be led by the Holy Spirit, we will step into God's abundant provision. But if we don't, we will never have enough because Father's provision is always at His place of positioning.

LITTLE KEYS TO ABUNDANT PROVISION

Key #11: Keep your eye on the prize, not the pits.

Questions for Reflection and Personal Application

1. Has God ever planted a dream in your heart? If so, what have you done to pursue it? Where are you, to your knowledge, on the path to its fulfillment?

2. Think about a goal you were pursuing (or are currently pursuing). Did you experience any opposition along the way? In what form? How did you deal with it? According to the Word of God, how should you deal with the distractions of the devil?

3. Think about a time when you needed to "kiss your comfort zone good-bye" in order to achieve something. What was the nature of the discomfort you experienced? What was the outcome?

Prayer

Ask God to reveal to you a dream He would have you pursue. Then open your heart to receive instructions from Him. Ask Him to give you the courage to step outside of your comfort zone as you go after the God-inspired dreams in your heart.

CHAPTER 12

"I WILL EQUIP YOU FOR YOUR APPOINTMENT"

For we are God's workmanship, created in Christ Jesus to do good works, which God prepared in advance for us to do.

—Ephesians 2:10

I have traveled a lot in my years of ministering. When Destiny was younger, I always carried a backpack filled with activities to keep her occupied in the car or on the airplane. I would go to the Dollar Store and purchase various things to entertain her. One of her favorite items was Silly Putty. We would play a game we called "Look What I Made," in which we took turns forming something we'd thought up and then asking the other person to guess what it was. We formed in our minds what we would make before shaping the Silly Putty according to that design.

That's the way it is with the Lord. Before He formed each of us, He knew us, and so He knew what He was doing when He made us. When He was creating you, He might have said, "I want this one to have a heart of compassion," or "This one is going to go all the way with Me without compromising," or "This one is going to preach My Word," or "This one will be a witness for Me in the corporate world." God knew just what He wanted you to do for His kingdom, and He formed you with the equipping you'd need to fit in that space. Every one of us was formed after God had known us and had figured out what He wanted us to do for Him.

Every one of us has been given gifts and talents to use for God's glory, according to our particular calling. Some people say, "But I don't have any talents." I remember thinking that very thing as a young Christian. And it's a lie from the pit of hell. Before long, the Lord told me that my strongest gift was the gift of determination. All along, I'd never thought determination counted as a gift! But the Lord said, "I gave you the gift you needed most—determination." Then, as I reflected on my life, He revealed to me how my determination had enabled me to overcome every obstacle and meet every challenge the enemy had thrown across my path in an attempt to hinder me from fulfilling my God-given purpose.

While some of us have traits we never acknowledged as gifts, others of us have hidden talents just waiting to be developed. When I first got saved, the last thing I could see myself doing was speaking in front of people. Public speaking was way outside of my comfort zone. But I soon learned that getting outside my comfort zone was a prerequisite to entering my "potential zone" in God.

As it turns out, the gift of public speaking was buried deep beneath all of the emotional baggage I'd carried since childhood, when my parents got divorced, an event that resulted in me growing up feeling insecure and easily intimidated by others. The Lord has done a lot of excavating in my life to uncover buried treasure. He has dug down deep, by the power of His Holy Spirit, and healed me to the point where the buried gifts and talents could be unearthed, dusted off, polished, and developed into their full

potential. You, too, have a buried treasure trove of gifts and talents the Lord wants to uncover for the sake of His kingdom. I say, let the excavation begin!

CREATED FOR A CALLING

The Lord told Jeremiah, *"Before you were born I set you apart; I appointed you as a prophet to the nations"* (Jer. 1:5). God set you apart long before you left your mother's womb to be born into the world. Maybe your birth came about as the result of rape. That doesn't make you a mistake! God is the *"author of life"* (Acts 3:15), yours included. You weren't an accident; you were created intentionally with a divine purpose!

James Robison, founder and president of LIFE Outreach International, is a man of God who is being used greatly for kingdom purposes. And he was born because his mother was raped. God is the giver of all life. Your mother didn't have to conceive, but God ordained that she would conceive—you! Even when Satan means something for evil, God can use it for His glorious good (see Gen. 50:20; Rom. 8:28).

God set you apart in your mother's womb, and He sets you apart from the world today, that you might realize His appointment for you. Unlike God, Satan is not all-knowing, but he knows enough to realize when you pose a potential threat to his kingdom of darkness. He knows that you have what it takes to put a huge dent in his fender. Trust me, Satan knows enough about your appointment to strategically scheme against it. So while God sets us apart from the womb, the enemy sets out to steal, to kill, and to destroy God's purposes for our lives (see John 10:10).

God told Jeremiah that he had been *"appointed"* as a prophet to the nations. That was his purpose. You, too, have an appointment with destiny. Self-appointment won't take us far in the kingdom of God, but God-appointments will.

LET GOD "SCHEDULE" YOUR APPOINTMENT

In the area of Virginia where I live, we have seven different cities, each with its own mayor. Over the years, I have seen many mayoral candidates who seem a lot less qualified than even my teenage nephew! One day, I was reading up on a particular candidate, and the Lord said to me, "Anyone can run for office, but not everyone can run the city." Can you imagine the chaos? That's what happens when we try to appoint ourselves to do something the Lord hasn't called us to do. He equips you for that to which He has called you. His call precedes His equipping, or His provision, which precedes His appointment. Don't self-appoint—you may just self-destruct!

If you're like me, you don't enjoy going to the dentist. Whenever we have an appointment that we aren't particularly excited about, it's tempting to reschedule indefinitely. Over the years, I have learned that there is never a convenient time to go to the dentist, so I may as well just go and get it over with. When it comes to fulfilling our God-given call, we may want to wriggle our way out of any appointments that threaten to drag us out of our comfort zones. But if we'll just decide to go for it, we'll always be glad we did! Our potential zone is worlds better than our comfort zone, but we won't know it until after we've stepped into it.

THE WAY TO PROVISION AND APPOINTMENT

No one is able to enter the Promised Land season of life until passing through the wilderness, at least for a time. It's all a part of the process; after all, God is a God of process. It's in the process that He does such a great work in us. He always has to do a work in us before He can do a work through us. However, our obedience is often what determines the timing and length of our season. Obedience causes us to keep our originally-scheduled appointment

with our destiny. Our disobedience delays that appointment. I was recently in Israel, and as I traveled across the desert into the land of Canaan, I witnessed firsthand how quick their trip really could have been. The children of Israel could have made it all the way into the Promised Land by foot in only eleven days, yet it took them forty years!

Talk about a delay! That was ridiculous; but if we aren't careful, the same thing can happen to us. We grumble, we complain, and right there in the season we don't like, we remain—for years! God has an appointed time for seasons in our lives, and our obedience causes us to keep our appointments.

Don't Miss Your Appointment

The prophet Jeremiah is a great example of one who kept his appointment with the Lord. Jeremiah 1:4-5 says,

The word of the LORD came to me, saying, "Before I formed you in the womb I knew you, before you were born I set you apart; I appointed you as a prophet to the nations."

First, we must *let* the Word of the Lord *come* to us when He wants to speak to us. We are great at hearing the Word of the Lord for others. We can sit in a service and think, *Wow! I wish so-and-so was here to hear this Word—she really needs it!* But the truth is, the Holy Spirit wants us to be open, and stay open, to His Word coming to us. The Holy Spirit wants to put His finger on things in our lives on a regular basis, but it takes us being open. If we have been walking with the Lord for any amount of time, we can think, *I already know that Scripture. I've heard it a million times.* And then, we can unconsciously tune out the *now* Word that the Lord wants to speak to us. We can miss the Holy Spirit's work in us when we don't let the word of the Lord come to us, which causes us to miss the appointment He has for our lives.

God told Jeremiah—and He's telling you today—*"Before I formed you...I knew you."* God knew what He needed you to do in His kingdom, and He formed you accordingly, so that you would make your appointment.

THE TRANSFORMATION PROCESS

God makes provision for our unique appointments by equipping us with distinctive personalities, aptitudes, gifts, and talents. We are created with "built-in" tools and skills to tackle whatever challenge comes our way. That's what happens during our formation in the womb.

During our earthly life, as we grow and mature, we undergo a transformation by the Holy Spirit, who sets us up for our appointments and leads us in such a way that we'll make it on time. So God the Father forms you, and God the Holy Spirit transforms you.

We are all formed for our appointment, but then the Holy Spirit puts the finishing touches on us so that we become qualified for that appointment. Preparation always precedes our final qualification. James 1:2-3 says, *"Consider it pure joy, my brothers, whenever you face trials of many kinds, because you know that the testing of your faith develops perseverance."* One way that the Holy Spirit puts His finishing touches on us is through trials. Yes, God allows us to go through trials so our faith may be tested. One of the greatest ways that our faith is tested is through times of financial hardship, because God wants to know that we trust in Him, not in a paycheck.

REFINED THROUGH THE FORGIVENESS OF SINS

Thanks to Adam and Eve, each of us was born with a sin nature. That inborn trait, coupled with all of the challenges particular to

180

us—childhood abuse, maybe, or growing up without knowing Christ—puts us in desperate need of a transformation. When we repent of our sins, we are forgiven and justified—transformed in our spiritual nature. And when we allow the Holy Spirit to heal our hearts and work through the junk that's built up there, we're transformed into people who are ready for their divine appointments.

PERFECTED BY PRACTICING PERSEVERANCE

In the Parable of the Sower, it says,

Those on the rock [those whose highest love and authority is Jesus Christ] *are the ones who receive the word with joy when they hear it, but they have no root. They believe for a while, but in the time of testing they fall away* (Luke 8:13).

There will always be a time of testing—it's how the Holy Spirit prepares us for our transformation. And we must not fall away. When perseverance comes into play, we don't fall away. *Persevere* is defined as "to persist in anything undertaken; maintain a purpose in spite of difficulty, obstacles, or discouragement; continue steadfastly." In spite of difficulty or opposition, we must press forward to our appointment. Persevering means refusing to give up! We must refuse to give up until we've reached our divine appointment.

James 1:4 says, *"Perseverance **must** finish its work so that you may be mature and complete, not lacking anything." Must* means there's no way around it—there are no shortcuts in God. If we won't persevere, we won't become mature and complete. Persevering in challenging circumstances, including times of financial hardship, is a must if we are going to be mature and completely prepared for our appointments.

If the testing of our faith develops perseverance, we would do well to welcome every test because we'll need plenty of perseverance to keep our appointments with our God-given destinies. We *know* this is true, as James said in verse 3, but we often forget what we know in the midst of our trials. That's when we must remind ourselves of what we know to be true. In the midst of a financial crisis—when the bills are due, when bankruptcy is on the horizon, when you're buried in debt—don't forget what you know: God will get you through, just as He has in the past, and He will bring you out stronger than you were before.

FINISHED BY FAITH

Let's return to the example of King Jehoshaphat.

Then Jehoshaphat stood up in the assembly of Judah and Jerusalem at the temple of the LORD in the front of the new courtyard and said, "O LORD, God of our fathers, are you not the God who is in heaven? You rule over all the kingdoms of the nations. Power and might are in your hand, and no one can withstand you. O our God, did you not drive out the inhabitants of the land before your people Israel and give it forever to the descendants of Abraham your friend?" (2 Chronicles 20:5-7)

In the midst of the battle, Jehoshaphat prayed a prayer in which he reminded himself, as well as those around him, what he already knew—God is all-powerful, and He would be faithful, just as He always had been.

On the way to the fulfillment of our appointment for God, we will face many challenges, including financial challenges. And a key to fulfilling our appointment is to be prepared and qualified, and we do this when we submit to the transformation process, allowing the Holy Spirit to develop our faith.

God tested Abraham to make sure that the fulfillment of his vision—or appointment—didn't mean more to him than the one who gave him the vision.

Some time later God tested Abraham. He said to him, "Abraham!" "Here I am," he replied. Then God said, "Take your son, your only son, Isaac, whom you love, and go to the region of Moriah. Sacrifice him there as a burnt offering on one of the mountains I will tell you about" (Genesis 22:1-2).

This was just one test in a series of many that God administered to Abraham. He had waited for many, many years for the fulfillment of the word God had given him. He knew about his appointment, and he'd even tried to speed up the process, but we know how that went—he wound up with Ishmael instead of with God's perfect plan. When he realized the futility in trying to bring God's plan to fruition in his own timing, Abraham stopped giving God his "help" and gave Him obedience, instead. To test the extent of his obedience, God put forth the command for Abraham to slay his son on the altar. After all of that waiting and the birth of his long-awaited son, Abraham was now supposed to kill him? Yes, if God asked him to. He needed to show that God held first place in his life—that Abraham would remain obedient to Him, no matter the cost. God never wants us to value anything or anyone above Him, for only when He is in first place can we say that we have no idols. He must be our first love and our highest allegiance.

When we pass the testing of our faith—which is kind of misleading, because it's a lifelong process—we become qualified for our regularly scheduled appointment with destiny. *"So, as the Holy Spirit says: 'Today, if you hear his voice, do not harden your hearts as you did in the rebellion, during the time of testing in the desert'"* (Heb. 3:7-8). The children of Israel hardened their hearts; therefore, most of them failed the test and never made it out of the desert into their destiny: the Promised Land. As much as God loves us, and as much as He wants us to keep our appointment with our destiny, the choice is up to us alone!

QUALIFIED BECAUSE OF SOUL-CONTROL

Third John 1:2 says, *"Beloved, I pray that you may prosper in all things and be in health, just as your soul prospers"* (NKJV). As we see in this verse, the condition of our soul affects every other area of our lives. Your soul contains your will, your emotions, and your mind. If your soul is not prospering in the Lord, it's hard for the other areas of your life to prosper. And your soul prospers only when you have what I call "soul-control." If your soul is not under the control of your spirit, you don't have soul-control. Instead, you are driven by the desires of your soul—what you want, what you think, and how you feel. That's a recipe for disaster! But if you keep your soul under the control of your spirit—a spirit that submits to the Lord—you put yourself in position to prosper in every area.

EXEMPLIFYING INTEGRITY

God wants to get us to the place where He can trust us with everything He has, including financial prosperity, the gifts of the Spirit, the power and wisdom of God, and the discernment of the Holy Spirit.

Joseph was first entrusted with Potiphar's house before he came into his own destiny—the house of Pharaoh. If we aren't first faithful over another person's vision, God can't entrust us with our own vision. We have to be prosperous in another person's house before God can entrust us with our own. God required me to be faithful over another person's vision—during the years that I came off the road and went home to serve my pastors—before He fully trusted me with my own call and vision.

During those years, God required me to prosper in another person's "house" before I could be promoted to my own "house," or vision. I never would have been promoted if I would not have been prosperous. What I mean by prosperous is fruitful. I did everything as unto the Lord with all of my heart. I did whatever

was required from me, and I did it with a standard of excellence. When I was given a job or a task, I took it to the next level. I didn't just do a half-hearted job; I gave it my all and did my very best. As a result, God blessed everything I put my hand to, and I was eventually promoted to pursue my own vision and call. Did I ever feel like quitting and leaving? Oh yeah—sometimes twice a day! But I proved my integrity and was blessed as a result.

Genesis 39:5 says,

From the time he put him in charge of his household and of all that he owned, the LORD blessed the household of the Egyptian because of Joseph. The blessing of the LORD was on everything Potiphar had, both in the house and in the field.

The favor of God on Joseph affected all of those who were around him. We are affected by those we associate with, and we affect those who associate with us. I don't know about you, but I like to hang out with those people who have the favor of God on them!

No one is greater in this house than I am. My master has with-held nothing from me except you, because you are his wife. How then could I do such a wicked thing and sin against God? And though she spoke to Joseph day after day, he refused to go to bed with her or even be with her (Genesis 39:9-10).

Joseph refused to compromise or even associate with someone who was willing to sin in such a flagrant way. Because of his integrity of character and uncompromising morals, Joseph prospered, even if he had to do a prison stint in the meantime. If we aren't thoroughly prepared, we can give God a bad name when we don't walk in Christ-like character as we represent Him.

Although Joseph passed the test in the eyes of God, it looked as if, once again, he was getting demoted. But remember, what goes up must go down. And the farther you go up, the farther you must go down.

Once again, Joseph was prosperous and was given a new level of favor. No matter what he went through, and no matter what happened to him, God supernaturally caused him to prosper!

Genesis 39:20-23 says,

Joseph's master took him and put him in prison, the place where the king's prisoners were confined. But, while Joseph was there in the prison, the LORD was with him; he showed him kindness and granted him favor in the eyes of the prison warden. So the warden put Joseph in charge of all those held in the prison, and he was made responsible for all that was done there. The warden paid no attention to anything under Joseph's care, because the LORD was with Joseph and gave him success in whatever he did.

God gave Joseph success in whatever he did. He didn't have to strive for it; he just walked in success because he was obedient and maintained integrity of character. Promotion always comes from the Lord (see Ps. 75:6). And God doesn't have a hiring freeze on; He's just looking for qualified applicants whom He can promote.

Genesis 40:2-3 states,

Pharaoh was angry with his two officials, the chief cupbearer and the chief baker, and put them in custody in the house of the captain of the guard, in the same prison where Joseph was confined.

Once again, God was strategically positioning Joseph for the palace. Who would have ever dreamed that Joseph would be positioned for the palace by being thrown into prison? God's ways are definitely higher than our ways (see Isa. 55:9).

PERFECTED THROUGH PATIENCE

While Joseph was in prison, the chief cupbearer and the chief baker each had a dream that was troublesome, and Joseph gave them

the interpretations (see Gen. 40). Afterward, Joseph told them, "When things go well with you, remember me." He wanted them to mention him to Pharaoh so he could get set free from the prison.

Two full years had passed, and Joseph was still in prison for a crime he had not committed. Meanwhile, God was doing a great work in him. Finally, Pharaoh had a dream, and the chief cup-bearer remembered Joseph and told Pharaoh about him. God's preparation process is often slow, but when God's appointed time comes, we are promoted and prospered in our purpose.

Genesis 41:14 says, *"So Pharaoh sent for Joseph, and he was quickly brought from the dungeon. When he had shaved and changed his clothes, he came before Pharaoh."* God wants us to be "clean-shaven"—ready and poised for our promotion.

If we seek God and obey His voice in His positioning process, we can be prosperous and eventually get promoted. But this process can take months, years, or even decades! We don't just receive the vision or dream from God one day and walk into the palace the next day. God doesn't just put you in charge overnight! If He did, it's likely you would self-destruct because of stress. You don't get your driver's license at two years old; you have to grow to a mature age and undergo thorough training. Then you must pass the test and get the stamp of approval from the authorities. Then and only then do you get your license. If you didn't do things the right way, you would be a danger to yourself and to everyone else.

Transformation Brings Us to Our Divinely Appointed Destination

Then Pharaoh said to Joseph, "Since God has made all this known to you, there is no one so discerning and wise as you. You shall be in charge of my palace, and all my people are to

187

submit to your orders. Only with respect to the throne will I be greater than you" (Genesis 41:39-40).

Joseph had grown in wisdom and discernment during his preparation time, and he was ready for his promotion. At God's appointed time, God restored to Joseph what was stolen from him, and even gave him more than double for his trouble. Genesis 41:42 says, *"Then Pharaoh took his signet ring from his finger and put it on Joseph's finger. He dressed him in robes of fine linen and put a gold chain around his neck."* Joseph now was given robes—plural. And it was all in God's timing.

Joseph saw the fulfillment of his vision and soon forgot all that he had been through. Genesis 42:6 says, *"Now Joseph was the governor of the land, the one who sold grain to all its people. So when Joseph's brothers arrived, they bowed down to him with their faces to the ground."* God knew the end from the beginning, and He was positioning Joseph for his purpose.

God really does position us to prosper, and when the enemy tries to get in there to steal, kill, and destroy, even though people close around us, God will give us double for our trouble if we keep our hearts right. The only thing that can steal God's call, will, and blessings from our lives is our own heart attitudes. People can't control your destiny unless you allow them to. You allow them to control your life and destiny when you respond with anger, bitterness, and unforgiveness.

Joseph loved his brothers and responded to their actions with a heart of forgiveness. He said to them, *"And now, do not be distressed and do not be angry with yourselves for selling me here, because it was to save lives that God sent me ahead of you"* (Gen. 45:5). Joseph recognized that it was the hand of God, not his own brothers. God used situations and circumstances to develop Christ-like character in Joseph and to position him for greatness!

You lack nothing that you need in order to go to the next level. I spent seven years in college and graduate school, and I often felt like one of the Israelites in the desert, surviving on "manna" of thirty-nine-cent tacos from Taco Bell. In those seven years, I built up my perseverance, which was essential for me to get where I was going. To earn my degrees, I needed every single credit that was required of me. I couldn't be lacking anything—not even a single credit! The same is true with God. If we want to graduate to the next level, we need to earn every credit, lacking nothing.

Right on Time for the Right Appointment

The Holy Spirit does His best to make sure you are on time and you arrive at the right appointment. Have you ever bent over backward to get to an appointment on time, only to find out you'd marked the wrong date on your calendar? I have! Talk about frustrating. It's not only important to arrive on time, but it's equally important to arrive at the right appointment. It doesn't help if I arrive at the dentist on time for my appointment on the wrong day or if I go on the right day to my physician's office expecting a dental exam. And it works the same way with our God-given appointments.

Several years ago, the daughter of one of my staff members graduated from nursing school. A large percentage of her classmates had been disqualified, and so her graduation class became smaller and smaller. This fact prompted me to pray, and the Lord revealed to me that some of her classmates had not been formed for the nursing profession. So it wasn't entirely bad that they didn't qualify to graduate! Maybe they were supposed to do something else. If we try to qualify for an appointment God didn't intend for us, we won't thrive in that self-appointment.

When we are determined not to miss our God-given appointment—when we submit to the Holy Spirit's transformation process and persevere through the entire thing—we will keep our appointments with destiny. After the work of the Holy Spirit has transformed us, we can step into the appointment that we were formed for, and there's nothing more satisfying than that!

ALLOW THE PROCESS TO REACH COMPLETION

Many years ago, while I was ministering and traveling full-time, the Lord told me to go home and serve my pastors. I assumed He meant for a few weeks—six, at the most. It ended up being several years. At one point, God said to me, "You are only half-baked. I'm putting you back in the oven so that you will be completely done." He didn't tell me He was about to turn up the heat! At least, not in so many words. Believe me, I got baked to the point of being well-done! But that's what I needed if I wanted to one day hear Him say, *"Well done, my good servant!"* (Luke 19:17). The process wasn't entirely fun, but it was worth it: In the end, I was *"mature and complete, not lacking anything"* I needed for my years in ministry to follow.

When we are in the midst of undergoing the process, we're often so uncomfortable that the last thing we can think about is relaxing. Yet that's the best thing we could do. We can't change the process that was designed to change us. As we relax, we yield to the work of the Holy Spirit and let Him have His way with our hearts, attitudes, minds, and wills.

CULTIVATE CHRIST-LIKE CHARACTER

Think back to Joseph. His process was long and painful! It ultimately led him to the palace, but he endured plenty of pit stops along the way—being betrayed by his brothers, shackled in slavery, and sentenced to prison for a crime he didn't commit. But it was part of the process that was tailor-made to transform him into the

190

man of God he would one day be. God is interested in where we are going—our destiny—but He is even more interested in who we will be when we get there. The process is designed to assure that we represent the character of Christ in our lives. Our gifting can take us to a place of destiny, but our character assures that we can maintain that place of destiny. Many people's gifts take them to a place that their character can't maintain. That wasn't the case for Joseph, and God doesn't want that to be the case for you and me, either.

STAY FOCUSED AND FLEXIBLE

In the midst of the transformation process, we must stay focused and flexible. Many people wander aimlessly through the process because they are focused on what's happening around them rather than on their destination. Others shut down when things don't go "according to plan"—the way they thought they should—rather than being open to God's will and adaptable to different situations. Relax and keep your eye on the finish. Focus and flexibility will speed up the transformation process and put you at a new level that much more quickly.

RELAX—YOU'RE IN PROCESS

Life is a process of tests and experiences God uses to shape us into the people He wants us to be. During that process, the Holy Spirit does a work in us so that God may do a work through us. Every person who has ever been used mightily by God has undergone this process.

God wants you to enjoy the process of pursuing His plans for your life, whether you're raising your children, working to prosper a ministry or business, or doing something else that's uniquely catered to the way you were created. If we aren't enjoying life and experiencing God, something is wrong. Often that "something" is a failure to relax as we go from one level to the next. You may as well relax, because you will be in some stage of process, for one reason or another, until you get to heaven. So relax and enjoy the trip!

ABIDE IN THE VINE AND ENJOY THE TIME

We can relax and enjoy the trip by daily abiding in the true Vine, Jesus Christ, who said,

> *Abide in Me, and I in you. As the branch cannot bear fruit of itself, unless it abides in the vine, neither can you, unless you abide in Me. I am the vine, you are the branches. He who abides in Me, and I in him, bears much fruit; for without Me you can do nothing* (John 15:4-5 NKJV).

Abide is defined as "to remain; continue; stay" and "to have one's abode; dwell; reside." We have the choice: Abide in the world, where we're subject to stress, burnout, and other pressures, or abide in the Lord, where we find a peaceful refuge. That seems like a no-brainer to me!

You get your strength, nourishment, and direction from whatever vine you are abiding in. Are you abiding in a vine other than the Lord? If so, don't expect it to sustain you for long. False vines produce false fruit in our lives: a false sense of security, a false sense of peace, a false sense of acceptance, a false sense of significance, and so on. But when we abide in the *"true vine,"* Jesus Christ—through prayer, worship, and the study of His Word—we will produce great fruit.

As we're abiding in the true vine, we submit to the pruning process, by which God removes every part of us that isn't bearing fruit (see John 15:1-2). *Prune* means "to rid or clear of (anything superfluous or undesirable)" and "to remove (anything considered

192

superfluous or undesirable)." Father God does the pruning so we can stop blaming those around us, even though He may use them to "[speak] *the truth in love*" (Eph. 4:15) to us about a particular "branch" that needs to be sawed off.

Many people don't like to submit to the pruning process, and they become prunes instead of getting pruned. They grow bitter and angry and become spiritually dried up, just like a prune in the natural. I want to challenge you not to become a spiritual prune, but to submit to the pruning process and allow God to produce great fruit in you and through you.

One night soon after my husband left me, I was sitting in my rocking chair with my newborn daughter, wondering when—if ever—I would fulfill the call I knew God had on my life. My prospects seemed slim, now that I was a single mom. I prayed, "Lord, when is my ministry going to grow?"

He quickly responded, "It's growing quicker than you think." (I knew He was referring to my daughter.) Then He added, "And for everything, there's a time. Just keep abiding in the vine." Whatever you are facing today, be encouraged: As you keep abiding in the vine, God's perfect timing will bring the fulfillment of your dreams.

LITTLE KEYS TO ABUNDANT PROVISION

Key #12: Abide in the vine and enjoy the time.

QUESTIONS FOR REFLECTION AND PERSONAL APPLICATION

1. What are some of the unique gifts and aptitudes God has given you? How are you putting them to use in

His kingdom? If you aren't sure, think about some ways you might serve others to the glory of God with your talents.

2. Consider the steps of the "Holy Spirit transformation process" outlined in this chapter (keeping in mind that these are just a sampling of the exhaustive work He does in our lives): forgiveness of sins, perseverance, faith, soul-control, integrity, and patience. How many of those steps have you submitted to? Is the fruit of those particular tests evident in your Christian walk today?

3. To what degree have you enjoyed the transformation process? How do you think you might increase your ability to relax, abide in the vine, and enjoy the time?

Prayer

Thank your heavenly Father for creating you with a specific purpose in mind, even if you aren't yet sure what that purpose is. Praise Him for the gifts and abilities He's given you, and ask Him to show you how He would have you use them in service to others and for His glory.

Chapter 13

"Nothing Will Be Impossible for You"

Nothing is impossible with God.

—Luke 1:37

Jesus said to him, "Receive your sight; your faith has healed you."

—Luke 18:42

If you believe, you will receive whatever you ask for in prayer.

—Matthew 21:22

Several years ago, the Holy Spirit was prompting me to expand our television ministry and broadcast on a different network. The weekly expense was going to be much greater than we had ever paid for airtime before. As I sought the Lord in fasting and prayer, He said to me, "You can't afford to miss this window of opportunity." In my natural mind, I had actually been thinking

I couldn't afford to pay the airtime bill. But God got in the middle of things and told me I couldn't afford to miss what He was leading me to do.

As I pondered in prayer what the Lord had said to me, I realized I needed to have "limitless thinking." God showed me that if I didn't do what He was leading me to do, the day *could* come when I would stand before Him, and He would show me all the lives that He had wanted to reach through my ministry on this network, but couldn't because I didn't believe He would pay the bill. That shook me! I jumped out of the boat, we purchased the airtime, and God paid the bill every single week!

So often we believe that God can and will do the seemingly impossible for others, but we have a hard time believing that He will do the miraculous for us and through us. We need to believe that God wants to do it—whatever miracle *it* is for us!

There are realms of life in which limits are important, such as our spending, our diets, our television viewing, our electronic usage, our speech, and so forth. But in other areas, we shouldn't set any limits. For example, through doubt and skepticism, we limit what we expect God to do for us, through us, and in us. Yet He can do anything! But we need to believe that in our hearts. We need to have "limitless thinking." How do we take the limits off of our thinking? By following Joshua 1:8:

> *Do not let this Book of the Law depart from your mouth; meditate on it day and night, so that you may be careful to do everything written in it. Then you will be prosperous and successful.*

This verse tells us how to be prosperous and successful. Our mouths, our meditations, and our actions make it or break it for us. If we speak the Word, think the Word, and do the Word, as Joshua 1:8 instructs us to, then we open ourselves up to "limitless thinking" and free God to make us prosperous and successful.

Proverbs 23:7 says, *"As* [a man] *thinks in his heart, so is he..."* (NKJV). If you want to become a limitless thinker, you need to change the thoughts you entertain, and you can do this by meditating primarily on the Word of God. For us to reach our full potential, we must cast off the limits we place on our thinking— on what we expect God to do or believe He can provide for us. Otherwise, our doubts will stand in the way of His miraculous works on our behalf.

WHAT HAVE YOU BEEN THINKING ABOUT THE LORD?

Limitless thinking enables us to possess all the promises of God for our lives. Limited thinking, on the other hand, causes us to doubt, and doubt hinders us from stepping out and possessing the promises. When God says it's time for something, we need to make sure our natural minds don't kick in and cause us to say, "No, thank You" to God. Limitless thinking prepares us to receive the promises of God because we receive them with faith, not doubt.

When Moses died, Joshua was promoted overnight. Joshua 1:2-3 says,

> *Moses my servant is dead. Now then, you and all these people, get ready to cross the Jordan River into the land I am about to give to them—to the Israelites. I will give you every place where you set your foot, as I promised Moses.*

The Lord told him, "It's your turn, buddy! Rise to the occasion; you're the man!"

Are you ready? Are you ready to cross over to a new level, a new position, a new anointing, and a new set of responsibilities? The word of the Lord to you is that you will lead the people and possess the land. Yes, you! Then He says in verse 3 that He will give you every place you set your foot. If you are sitting down on the sidelines and you refuse to get up and take a step of faith because of your limited thinking, you could miss the greatest window of opportunity that you will ever have.

We have to be ready so that when God says, "Now!" we can act. Don't allow your current financial situation to limit you and confine your thinking. The truth is, God owns it all. You have to take the step of faith before you inherit anything! It's nothing for Him to provide when you are doing what He has told you to do. Now, if you jump out of the boat before He bids you to come, you might get wet instead of walking. But God knows your heart, and He will catch you if you get a bit ahead of Him.

RESIST THE SPIRITS OF LACK AND LIMITATION

When we find ourselves in challenging financial circumstances—when we find ourselves out of our comfort zones—we must resist the spirits of lack and limitation. First and foremost, don't limit God. God can always do exceedingly, abundantly above all you can think, ask, or even imagine (see Eph. 3:20). The spirit of limitation not only limits God, but it limits what you "think" God can do in you, through you, and for you.

James 4:7 says, *"Submit yourselves, then, to God. Resist the devil, and he will flee from you."* When we do our part of James 4:7, God will do His, and the devil and his unclean spirits will flee. The spirits of lack and limitation are two unclean spirits that try to attack God's people and prevent them from going forward. If we allow ourselves to entertain thoughts that originate from the spirit of lack or limitation, we can easily be distracted, discouraged, and tempted to quit. But when we resist them with the Word of God—the truth—they will flee, and we can maintain the mindset of the Lord, which says, "I know my God can do it. For Him, there's nothing to it!"

Escape the Delusions of Limited Thinking

Limited thinking can cause us to get emotional, delusional, and even downright ridiculous about the way we view things. We see the perfect example of this in Deuteronomy 1:27-28:

You grumbled in your tents and said, "The LORD hates us; so he brought us out of Egypt to deliver us into the hands of the Amorites to destroy us. Where can we go? Our brothers have made us lose heart. They say, 'The people are stronger and taller than we are, the cities are large, with walls up to the sky. We even saw the Anakites there.'"

They started thinking and even saying, "The Lord hates us." Get real! Talk about being emotional! This was definitely a spirit of limitation trying to control their thoughts and minds. Have you ever experienced difficult times—the loss of a job, foreclosure on a house—and said, "The Lord must hate me"? If so, may I suggest you employ some soul-control at that very moment and don't yield to the spirit of limitation? Get a grip on yourself and remind yourself of everything God has done for you in the past.

The Israelites were freaking out! They looked in the natural and focused on how big the enemy seemed to be. They said that the walls of the city were up to the sky—an exaggeration, of course, brought about by their fearful mindset. They went on to say, "We even saw the Anakites there." Oooooohhh, not the Anakites! Who cares if the Anakites were there? God is bigger than the Anakites! And He's on your side, not theirs.

When you are up against that financial mountain—when the bank or the creditors seem so big—remember that God is the ruler of the universe of which they are a part. Nothing has changed except your circumstances. God is still on His throne, and He doesn't have to hock the pearly gates of heaven to pay your bills.

All He requires is your obedience. So stop looking with natural eyes and having meltdowns every time you turn around.

Deuteronomy 1:30-31 says,

The LORD your God, who is going before you, will fight for you, as he did for you in Egypt, before your very eyes, and in the desert. There you saw how the LORD your God carried you, as a father carries his son, all the way you went until you reached this place.

God had fought for the children of Israel in Egypt before, and He was going to fight for them again. Just as God had carried them before, He was going to carry them again. I want to challenge you today to get rid of limited thinking and focus on the fact that the Lord is going before you. The Lord is carrying you—and will continue to carry you—until you reach your destination, or your destiny in Him. You must get rid of the spirit of limitation, or you will lose the battle unnecessarily.

Deuteronomy 1:32-33 says,

In spite of this, you did not trust in the LORD your God, who went ahead of you on your journey, in fire by night and in a cloud by day, to search out places for you to camp and to show you the way you should go.

In spite of everything the Lord had done for them in the past, they still didn't trust Him. They allowed a spirit of limitation to overtake them, and they were in danger of losing the battle as a result.

Deuteronomy 1:42 says, *"But the LORD said to me, 'Tell them, "Do not go up and fight, because I will not be with you. You will be defeated by your enemies."'"* We can't go to battle with a spirit of limitation, or we will be defeated. We must take the limits off. We must have limitless thinking.

200

CAST OFF THE SELF-IMPOSED LIMITATION
OF AGE

When I was just a twenty-one-year-old traveling evangelist, the enemy would try to intimidate me with the fact that I was so young. Of course, I have seen many people give up their God-inspired pursuits because they thought they were too old. The devil will come up with whatever he can to try to stop you in your tracks. Don't buy his lies! Joseph was only seventeen when God gave him his vision; Moses was...well, really, really old; but God used them both greatly for His kingdom purposes. The Lord will use you when it's time, no matter your age.

> *The word of the LORD came to me, saying, "Before I formed you in the womb I knew you, before you were born I set you apart; I appointed you as a prophet to the nations." "Ah, Sovereign LORD," I said, "I do not know how to speak; I am only a child." But the LORD said to me, "Do not say, 'I am only a child.' You must go to everyone I send you to and say whatever I command you. Do not be afraid of them, for I am with you and will rescue you," declares the LORD* (Jeremiah 1:4-8).

You need to let the word of the Lord come to you today, just as it came to Jeremiah so many centuries ago. God knew you before He formed you, and He formed you with a special appointment—a divine destiny—in mind. You are fully equipped to fulfill the assignment He designed just for you, and He knows how young or how old you are. Stop making excuses and putting off your appointment!

Jeremiah protested that he was too young, but God told him to forget about his age. Stop making your youth or years more of an issue than they need to be! Maintain limitless thinking and keep on keeping on.

WHAT HAVE YOU BEEN SAYING OF THE LORD?

"I will say of the Lord, He is my Refuge and my Fortress, my God; on Him I lean and rely, and in Him I [confidently] trust!" (Ps. 91:2 AMP). It's important to be aware of what we are "saying" of the Lord. On occasion, the Lord has said to me, "Danette, you need a mouth makeover!" What He means is, "You need to *'say of the LORD'* what is true." We should be like the psalmist and call the Lord our *"Refuge and Fortress."* We should be proclaiming that we confidently trust in Him. Yet more often than we realize, we say the opposite of what we ought to. We whine and say things like, "This isn't fair. Why do I have to go through this? Why, God? How come I have it so hard, while everybody else has it easy?" Blaming the Lord for our miserable situation or merely lamenting our state while ignoring the promises that belong to all of God's children, paints an inaccurate portrait of the One we claim to trust in.

Psalm 37:23 says, *"The steps of a good man are ordered by the LORD, and He delights in his way"* (NKJV). If God is your Savior, then your steps have been ordered by Him. Any complaining you do might as well be directed at Him. God is in control; He hasn't left His throne, even if your house is about to be foreclosed or your electricity is about to be shut off. Even in the worst situations imaginable, the Lord is in control, and we can trust Him to bring us through. But we need to believe that—and our words should reflect our belief! Say of the Lord what is right—what His Word tells you is true—and you will maintain a proper perspective in every circumstance.

When we sit in a chair, we are making a statement of faith—faith that the piece of furniture will bear our weight. When we lean on the Lord, we make a different statement of faith, either verbally or through our actions, that we're trusting Him to hold us up. Proverbs 3:5-6 says,

Trust in the LORD with all your heart and lean not on your own understanding; in all your ways acknowledge him, and he will make your paths straight.

When we lean on our own understanding, the outcome can be disastrous! Our own understanding is based in the realm of our soul, which encompasses the will, mind, and emotions. If there's one thing that's apt to mislead us, it's our soul. What we need is soul-control—a soul that's subject to our spirit, which is yielded to the Lord. When our spirits, which have been renewed by the Lord (see Ps. 51:10), control our souls and our flesh, we are able to lean joyfully and confidently on our heavenly Father rather than on our own limited understanding.

ACKNOWLEDGE YOUR BELIEF IN GOD

In chapter 20 of Second Chronicles, a group of men rushed to inform King Jehoshaphat, *"A vast army is coming against you,"* and they aren't all that far away (2 Chron. 20:2). *Vast* was kind of an understatement. This humongous army was after Jehoshaphat, and they were advancing with alarming speed. It's one thing when a storm is coming, but it's something else altogether when it's the size of Texas! Yet the Word tells us that, while Jehoshaphat was alarmed (see 2 Chron. 20:3), he didn't react out of his flesh, but out of his spirit. He called for the nation to fast as they called on the Lord for help.

When we react out of our flesh, we tend to freak out—we cry, scream, yell, and emit other unproductive responses. Some people react out of their flesh by running away from the situation and from God, even if they've never needed God more. Jehoshaphat, however, was spiritually mature, and he reacted out of his spirit. In the midst of the biggest battle of his life, he didn't cry or run away. Despite the alarm he must have experienced, he inquired of the Lord. He didn't react by running in a panic to his friends, his family, his pastor, or his boss. Instead, he acted—he came before the Lord in fasting and in prayer—and his example of calm composure encouraged those around him to do the same.

So many times, we make an immediate, emotionally-charged response to the crisis at hand. Emotional reactions are a waste of time and energy, and they do nothing to help the situation. In fact, they usually make matters worse. Instead of reacting to the battle ahead by acknowledging how big and powerful the enemy is, act out of your spirit by stepping back and proclaiming, "My God is bigger and more powerful than my fiercest foe, and with His help, I can defeat whatever enemy comes against me."

Jehoshaphat did just that. Instead of running away, he ran straight to the Lord to seek the battle plan he believed He would provide. Through prayer and fasting, Jehoshaphat and the people of his kingdom sought the wisdom of all-powerful and almighty God. And the king's response set the tone for the people: They responded according to his example. If Jehoshaphat had panicked and come unglued, utter bedlam would have broken out as everyone else did the same thing. And a kingdom in disarray doesn't stand a chance against an attacking army. When we react out of our emotions, we lower our defenses and make ourselves vulnerable to the enemy's assaults. But if we act out of our spirits—if we say, "God, what's the plan?"—we leave no room for the enemy to gain a foothold. *If God is for us, who can be against us?*" (Rom. 8:31). When God is on our side, we always come out victors.

ACKNOWLEDGE GOD BEFORE OTHERS

When the people of Judah gathered at the temple, Jehoshaphat stood up and led them in prayer. He began,

> *O LORD, God of our fathers, are you not the God who is in heaven? You rule over all the kingdoms of the nations. Power*

and might are in your hand, and no one can withstand you
(2 Chronicles 20:6).

When we acknowledge God for who He is, we don't have any trouble leaving Him in control of our situation. But when we forget who God is and what He is ready to do on our behalf, it's easy to grapple for control and try to fix things in our own strength.

Jehoshaphat didn't have this problem because he immediately acknowledged God as the sovereign, omnipotent Lord He is. In so doing, he looked to God for his solution, and rightly so. We, too, need to acknowledge the Lord, the omniscient One, as our anchor in the midst of our battles. It's all too easy to get so distracted by the size of the army that's coming against us and to forget how much bigger and stronger our God is.

When we panic, we try to do in the flesh what can only be done in the Spirit. Let me tell you: If a vast army was coming against you, and you failed to recognize God and His abilities, you would lose your peace, your joy, and eventually, your battle. When we get in the flesh, we can try to do things ourselves; we claim the battle as our own. But when we realize who God is, even in the midst of our circumstances, we can let God remain in control.

As Jehoshaphat continued his prayer, he brought to remembrance everything that God had already done for his people. He said to the Lord,

> *O our God, did you not drive out the inhabitants of this land before your people Israel and give it forever to the descendants of Abraham your friend? They have lived in it and have built in it a sanctuary for your Name, saying, "If calamity comes upon us, whether the sword of judgment, or plague or famine, we will stand in your presence before this temple that bears your Name and will cry out to you in our distress, and you will hear us and save us"* (2 Chronicles 20:7-9).

When we bring to remembrance all that the Lord has done for us in the past, it builds faith in us to face our current situation. As we thank God for His past provision, offering up examples of times when He's come through for us, we encourage ourselves and build up our faith.

ACKNOWLEDGE GOD'S TRACK RECORD OF PROVISION

I have many testimonies of God's miraculous provisions for me personally and for my ministry that I call upon when the doubts start to sneak up on me. When I come up against a financial struggle, I start praying and thanking God for all of the times He has provided for me in the past. When you think about it, you'll realize that God has never let you down. And He's never going to. I can't say it enough: Keep on reminding yourself of God's faithfulness in the past as you stand on His promises for today.

WHAT HAVE YOU BEEN ENVISIONING?

During the days of extreme lack as a single mom, I had to envision myself on the other side of my current season. The fact is, I was believing God for each diaper and every jar of baby food—daily! But I was determined that my faith was going to change the facts and transform my financial situation. The Lord kept telling me that I needed to "see" myself in a place of abundance. As mentioned previously, when you have been living on corn dogs and tuna fish for eighteen months, it's a little challenging to see the pathway out of the wilderness and on to the Promised Land. But that's where obedience came into play for me. The Lord put it on my heart to go to the nicest mall in our community to window shop. I would treat myself to a chocolate bar and walk around

206

saying, "Thank You, Lord, that the day is coming when I will be able to come to this mall and buy anything I want."

At the time, it seemed crazy, because I didn't have more than $20 to last me until the end of the month. But I needed to see myself, through faith, in a place of blessing. The atmosphere of the mall gave me a different picture from my surroundings at home, where the cupboards were bare and even the toilet paper had to be rationed.

I am happy to report that I now could shop at the mall on a regular basis, if I chose to. I am always frugal with my spending, so I don't go on shopping sprees, but if I truly need something, to obtain it is no longer a major obstacle, praise God. If we hang on to hope and refuse to park in the pit of lack, the shift in our financial season will be right around the corner.

What You See Is What You Get

No matter what sort of financial season you are in today, make sure you prepare for future seasons. If you think this season is your final destination, it probably will be. You have to see yourself blessed and prosperous, and that's a very important way that you prepare for your future season of abundance—you must see it!

In Genesis 13:14-15, the Lord said to Abraham, *"Lift up your eyes from where you are and look north and south, east and west. All the land that you see I will give to you and your offspring forever."* God said, "Okay. What you can see, I will give you." Abraham had to see it before he could possess it, and the same is true for us. If we can't see ourselves living in a season of abundance, we will probably never make it to the land of more than enough. But if we can see it, God will give it to us, because He desires to shower us with abundant blessings!

Acknowledging the Lord in all of our ways, as we're instructed to do in Proverbs 3:6, keeps us from acknowledging our circumstances—how dire they are and how they'll "never work out." When we acknowledge the Lord alone, we remain confident that He will see us through, no matter how impossible our situation seems.

See Yourself Successful

God is always telling me that my goals are too small. Why? Because all too often, I limit God, and I limit myself. Moses and Joshua both limited God and themselves, and as a result, they had a hard time conceiving their God-given goals! We often believe that God can do it for others and that God can do it through others, but we need to have the revelation that God can and will do it through us and for us!

Exodus 3:9-10 says,

And now the cry of the Israelites has reached me, and I have seen the way the Egyptians are oppressing them. So now, go. I am sending you to Pharaoh to bring my people the Israelites out of Egypt.

Moses had a list of reasons a mile long why he couldn't do what God was calling him to do. But God said, "I am sending you." When the great I Am sends you, trust me, you can do all things! It's when you are sending yourself that you are going to have a problem.

We see many examples in the Bible where people experienced a temporary delay on the way to the fulfillment of their dreams and visions, but the key word here is *temporary!* You may be temporarily delayed, but you are still destined! You are destined to win because you and God are the majority, and you are destined for the finish line of your God-inspired goals!

FOCUS ON THE FULFILLMENT OF YOUR GOALS

Maybe one of your goals is to be debt-free. Maybe one of your goals is to experience financial freedom. Well don't allow anything to stop you. Getting out of debt is a little bit like losing weight. You have to stay focused on the goal every day, all day. When I want to lose a few pounds, and I see myself approaching my goal, I sometimes go celebrate with a hot fudge sundae—not smart! I can waste all of my hard work in one day, because after the celebration starts, I want to party all day. So I get in "reward" mode. I'm rewarding myself with my next favorite comfort food, and before I know it, I've regained the five pounds I had lost.

The same is true with getting out and staying out of debt. Every choice you make must be focused on that goal. Don't reward yourself with a purchase. Reward yourself in other ways. Do activities with your family and friends that are free. Some of the best times I have ever had with my daughter have been things that didn't cost me five cents.

If your goal is to be debt-free, you must change your mindset and your spending habits. This will take a lot of discipline—the same necessary ingredient needed to lose weight, meet your business goals, maintain a powerful prayer life, and so forth.

Discipline is so important in our lives that Proverbs 5:23 actually says, *"He will die for lack of discipline, led astray by his own great folly."* We can actually die for lack of self-discipline. I believe we can die spiritually, and we can even die physically if we don't learn to control our flesh.

God wants us to be self-controlled so the Spirit, and not our flesh, is in control of our lives. And we can achieve this when we see ourselves as controlled by the Spirit and clothed in the character of Christ.

SEE YOURSELF AS STRONG AND COURAGEOUS

When Joshua was suddenly promoted as the leader of the Isra-elites, I'm sure he found his new role a little overwhelming at first. I'm sure he felt far from his comfort zone, even though he had been trained as Moses' assistant. Being second in command and being the head honcho are two completely different ball games. Overnight, God can thrust us into a new position. Even though we may not "feel" ready, we can rest assured that, with God, we are. Yes, we may need to lean on the Lord to a greater degree than ever before, but that's all part of it. God sets us up to be totally dependent on Him—that's how we grow. If we aren't willing to say good-bye to our comfort zones, we will never enter into our potential zones.

Every promotion that the Lord gives us comes with a new level of responsibility, and we need to take that responsibility seriously. We need to see ourselves fulfilling that responsibility to the best of our equipping. Joshua wasn't going to just get the land that Moses had; he was called to go to a whole new level. We don't just auto-matically possess the land that our parents and leaders possessed; we have to pay the price ourselves. You can't just have a relation-ship with God through your parents or your spiritual leaders—it has to be between you and God!

And then, God wants you to take it to a new level, a new place, a new dimension. God told Joshua that he was to accept this new responsibility to lead the people into the Promised Land. And that responsibility was going to take discipline, diligence, and determi-nation on Joshua's part.

Limited thinking causes you to stay in your box. Limited thinking kills your faith and hinders your growth. But limitless thinking causes you to know that no one can successfully come against you or thwart what God has called you to do.

God told Joshua to just relax, to be strong and courageous in Him, and to get ready for the greatest season of success that he would ever experience. And I believe that the Lord is saying the same thing to you today!

> *No one will be able to stand up against you all the days of your life. As I was with Moses, so I will be with you; I will never leave you nor forsake you. Be strong and courageous, because you will lead these people to inherit the land I swore to their forefathers to give them. Be strong and very courageous. Be careful to obey all the law my servant Moses gave you; do not turn from it to the right or to the left, that you may be successful wherever you go* (Joshua 1:5-7).

The Lord kept telling Joshua to be strong and courageous, over and over again. And then, He said, *"Be strong and **very** courageous."* When you tell your children the same thing three times in one conversation, you are trying to make sure they get it.

When God told Joshua to be strong and courageous, it was for a reason. God knew that Joshua was going to face some opposition along the way, and He wanted him to be ready for it. God does the same thing with us. If we are living a life of prayer, communicating with the Lord on a regular basis, He will often give us a heads-up concerning what's coming our way.

He wants us to be prepared. He wants us to be courageous and not caught off guard. When we have to face or deal with something dangerous, difficult, or even emotionally painful, He doesn't want us to withdraw from it. He wants us to face it head-on with the grace, the strength, and the power of the Holy Spirit.

We have to remember that if it was easy, everyone would be doing it. Possessing the land, doing the work of the Lord, and taking a stand for righteousness isn't always easy. But we will always succeed when we do it God's way. Verse 7 tells us to obey *all* the law. This is not an "obedience buffet" where you pick and choose what you will obey from day to day. We must eat all of the Word, not just the desserts. *All* means "all" in Hebrew and Greek, just as in English! Then it says, *"Do not turn from it."* In other words, stay on course—do what you know to do.

UNLIMITED DISCIPLINE, DILIGENCE, AND DETERMINATION

When it comes to your vision and goals, discipline gets you started, diligence will see you through the times of potential discouragement, and determination will ensure the successful completion of your goals. In other words, you are going to need a lot of determination to take you all the way to the finish line. There are many starters in life—many people who start out to reach their goals. But there are very few finishers—those who stay determined to see their goals, no matter what the cost, no matter what the opposition. All three of the "D's" must be employed at all times. As I said before, the formula for great success is discipline, diligence, and determination.

Disciplined means having or exhibiting "behavior in accord with rules of conduct; behavior and order maintained by training and control." *Diligent* is defined as "constant in effort to accomplish something; attentive and persistent in doing anything." *Determined* means "resolute; staunch; decided; settled; resolved." As we remain disciplined, diligent, and determined, we can see our goals become reality.

Hebrews 6:12 says, *"We do not want you to become lazy, but to imitate those who through faith and patience inherit what has been promised."* We have to be determined to maintain limitless faith and to exhibit limitless patience. That way, we will inherit what has been promised to us.

Remember Romans 4:18-21:

Against all hope, Abraham in hope believed and so became the father of many nations, just as it had been said to him, "So shall your offspring be." Without weakening in his faith, he faced the fact that his body was as good as dead—since he was about a hundred years old—and that Sarah's womb was also dead. Yet he did not waver through unbelief regarding the promise of God, but was strengthened in his faith and gave glory to God being fully persuaded that God had power to do what he had promised.

Abraham was fully persuaded. When you are fully persuaded, it births what I call Holy-Ghost-determination! When you are fully persuaded that God has the power to do what He has promised, you don't take no for an answer. Your Holy-Ghost-determination doesn't quit. Your Holy-Ghost-inspired determination presses your way past any obstacle, distraction, or possible times of discouragement because you know God has called you to greatness. When you are a person who is called to greatness, you can see the finish line (where God wants you to go), but there are seasons where you can't see how in the world you are going to get there! People who are called to greatness can get discouraged during these times if they don't remain *fully* persuaded.

The purpose of limitless thinking—of unlimited discipline, diligence, and determination—is not to keep us out of trouble and opposition, but to carry us through those difficult times. We must always be prepared for opposition, and when we believe that nothing is impossible for us, because of the omnipotent power of God in us, we can conquer any challenge that comes our way!

LITTLE KEYS TO ABUNDANT PROVISION

Key #13: Take the limits off of your thinking.

Questions for Reflection and Personal Application

1. What are some of the limits you tend to put on your thinking? Age? Resources? Experience? Education? Ask God to help you cast off those limits so that you may believe Him when He says that "nothing shall be impossible for you."

2. Do you tend to suspect that God is angry with you when things go wrong? Think through your reactions to adverse situations, and then, the next time you face something difficult, call to mind Scripture verses that speak to the contrary. A good example is Hebrews 4:15: *"For we do not have a high priest who is unable to sympathize with our weaknesses, but we have one who has been tempted in every way, just as we are—yet was without sin."*

3. There is power in the act of acknowledging God before others. Have you ever done so? If not, consider professing your faith to someone publicly.

4. When faced with financial hardship, do you tend to view the future as an unending road of the same? If so, you need to envision something else! Picture yourself out of debt. Paint a picture of the life you want to live, and pray that God would give you faith to see it become a reality.

Prayer

Discuss with God any limits on your thinking that have held you back from pursuing His best for you. Then, ask Him to give you a vision for your future—a vision that seems impossible—and proclaim your belief that He will make it a reality in your life.

CHAPTER 14

"WAIT ON ME, AND I WON'T LET YOU DOWN"

The LORD longs to be gracious to you; he rises to show you compassion. For the LORD is a God of justice. Blessed are all who wait for him!

—Isaiah 30:18

The apostle Paul exhorted believers to *"take up the whole armor of God, that you may be able to withstand in the evil day, and having done all, **to stand**"* (Eph. 6:13 NKJV). What does "having done all" entail? I believe everyone's situation is a little different, but all of our situations have similar requirements: obedience, prayer, fasting, and worship. After you have done everything the Lord has instructed you to do concerning your situation—after you have prayed, fasted, and worshiped Him—you have done all. But we need to do all every day that we are in the season of standing. You can't just pray for two days and walk in obedience for thirty-six hours and then say, "I'm done." No, you're not! You have to "do all" every day of your season if you are going to stand successfully.

Standing Successfully

The children of Israel wavered from time to time. Sometimes they stood on the Word, and other times they didn't. For us to be successful, we must learn the art of standing. And then, after we have done everything, we need to keep on standing.

I believe many of you reading this book are in a season of standing. I say season because you have been required to stand more than a day or two. We can all handle standing for twenty-four hours or maybe even as much as thirty-six hours, but after that—the fun's over!

When you are standing, make sure that you aren't standing in God's way with your disobedience. Also make sure you don't let anything or anyone stand between you and God as you are attempting to successfully stand in the midst of your situation.

Wait Patiently

Waiting is another very important part of standing. No one likes this part, including me! Actually, this is my least-favorite part. I'm not too bad at all the other parts, but waiting? That's a different story!

Often, when God says, "Stand still and wait," we are even more like fidgety children who can't keep still. We just have to be doing something! My daughter's favorite show is *America's Funniest Home Videos*. So many of the home videos are of wedding ceremonies at which the flower girl or the ring bearer just couldn't stand still. They pull over a potted plant, lie down on the steps of the altar, or start talking when they aren't supposed to. We can be a lot like that! We don't want to wait, but waiting is a vital part of standing.

218

RESIST THE TEMPTATION TO HELP GOD

Have you ever been tempted to try to help God? I learned years ago that God doesn't need my help; all He needs is my obedience. I know, because I tried to help Him once, and He said, "No, thanks!" Whether I like His instructions or not, obedience is what He requires.

If we try to help God, we'll get frustrated because we'll quickly discover that we're in over our heads. In fact, our meddling often makes a mess of things and usually prolongs our waiting time.

Abraham and Sarah both got tired of waiting, so they decided to help God. He had promised to give them a son, but both of them were getting up in age, and nothing was happening. So Sarah told Abraham to lie with her maidservant, Hagar. Not a good idea! The result was the birth of Ishmael, who was less than God's best. When you try to speed up the process by "helping God," you will always end up with an Ishmael. God's best is always worth waiting for.

BUILD FAITH WHILE YOU WAIT

The times when we're asked to stand on God's promises while we're awaiting their fulfillment are designed by God to test and to strengthen our faith.

James 1:2-4 says,

Consider it pure joy, my brothers, whenever you face trials of many kinds, because you know that the testing of your faith develops perseverance. Perseverance must finish its work so that you may be mature and complete, not lacking anything.

When we submit to these tests of faith, we develop perseverance. To *persevere* is "to persist in anything undertaken; maintain a purpose in spite of difficulty, obstacles, or discouragement;

219

continue steadfastly." Perseverance is a vital quality to develop in order to mature as Christians and be equipped to fulfill our calling. We can't just quit when things get difficult. We have to persevere and keep standing because there are many starters in life, but few finishers. It's easy enough to start something, but staying in the race until you've reached the finish line is something altogether different. If you are going to stand and keep on standing, you must learn to persevere, and perseverance is learned through the testing of your faith.

TRUST IN GOD'S TIMING

It took me a little while, but I learned that God is never late. He's rarely early, but He's never late! I don't know about you, but I like early. I'm one of those people who can't stand to be late. I get stressed if there's even the remotest chance that I'm going to be late. I run around, getting myself all worked up—for nothing, most of the time. Not only do I not like being late, but I like to arrive at least a few minutes early. That way, I don't stress myself out over the possibility of being late! But God is an on-time God. Don't allow yourself to get stressed out thinking He's going to be late, because it isn't possible for Him to be late. His timing is perfect, and He wants you to place your faith in Him to come through for you, even if it seems to be just in the nick of time.

AT THE PEAK OF YOUR IMPATIENCE, IT'S TURNAROUND TIME!

God is a God who moves at the speed of suddenly. Suddenly, things change. Suddenly we move from the season of winter into the season of spring. The new season may not look or feel any different at first, but the calendar tells us it's a new season. I want

to encourage you today. Even if the weather in the spirit seems as though it's still winter, it's not. The calendar says you are in a new season—the season of spring headed into the season of summer. Things are about to change, and they are about to change suddenly! Overnight, things change. Overnight, we are in a new season. And overnight, you too will be in a new season.

The pressure you have been feeling, the discomfort you have been going through, is because your season is changing. Father is turning things around for you. You feel pressure when the baby is positioned for delivery. You feel like you can't go another day because of the pressure. The baby is beginning to turn around. The baby is being positioned for birth. This word, this dream, this vision that you have been carrying is about to be birthed. God is getting you positioned for delivery.

TURNAROUND TIME CORRESPONDS WITH GOD'S TIMETABLE

Turnaround time doesn't come until you've carried that baby to term. Father is the only one who can turn that baby around. Standing on your head doesn't work. Nothing you do will work—Father is the only One who can do it. You can't speed things up, and you can't slow things down. Suddenly that baby is born, and your life will never be the same again.

Galatians 4:4-5 says, *"But when the time had fully come, God sent his Son, born of a woman, born under law, to redeem those under law, that we might receive the full rights of sons."* When time had fully come, God sent Jesus—not a day early or a day late. Father is the only One who knows when events should occur and orchestrates them accordingly—the birth of a vision, the dream of a future, the fulfillment of your goals, and so forth. But when the time has fully come, suddenly God turns everything around!

This is what the LORD says—the Redeemer and Holy One of Israel—to him who was despised and abhorred by the nation, to the servant of rulers: "Kings will see you and rise up, princes will see and bow down, because of the LORD, who is faithful, the Holy One of Israel, who has chosen you" (Isaiah 49:7).

Because God is faithful, He was totally turning things around in this passage. And because God is faithful to you and because He has chosen you, He is totally turning things around for you and your circumstances today.

Turnaround Time Initiates the Season of "Suddenlies"

Turnaround time always comes at the beginning of the season of "suddenlies." That's very important for you to understand. In the beginning of the season of suddenlies, you usually experience turnaround time first! In the season of suddenlies, there are no more disappointments. Again, Proverbs 13:12 says, *"Hope deferred makes the heart sick, but a longing fulfilled is a tree of life."* In the season of suddenlies, the desires or longings of your heart are fulfilled, and it truly is a tree of life. When the longing is fulfilled, it revives, encourages, and strengthens you.

Suddenly!

I believe God is working behind the scenes to set the stage for your suddenly! If you aren't expecting your suddenly, you won't be prepared when the time comes. When you are in the season of suddenlies, suddenly your dreams and visions come to pass. Suddenly you are promoted. Suddenly everything God has told you was going to happen begins to happen. Suddenly!

Ruth 2:13 says,

May I continue to find favor in your eyes, my lord," she said.
"You have given me comfort and have spoken kindly to your
servant—though I do not have the standing of one of your ser-
vant girls.

Though Ruth did not have the position, her character and
favor opened the door for her suddenly. During the season of suddenlies, people who had the "position" suddenly lose it overnight
due to poor character. And suddenly, those who didn't have the
"position," but have the character, get it! Ruth didn't have the
position, but she obtained the position and favor because of her
godly character.

When you are in the season of suddenlies, suddenly, everything
that you have done in secret gets rewarded outwardly. Suddenly
people begin to notice you. Suddenly you find favor in the eyes of
those in high places. And suddenly you are not only working in
the field, but you own it! Before long, Ruth married into the blessings, and she owned the field.

When you find favor with the Lord in the season of suddenlies,
suddenly everything that belongs to Him becomes yours! Suddenly
you go from the bottom to the top. Suddenly the last are first, and
the first have taken the backseat! Suddenly you are promoted!

Sudden Influx of the Enemy's Schemes

Just as you are entering into the season of suddenlies, the
enemy tries everything to distract and discourage you. He knows
that you are approaching the finish line to your dream and vision,
so he begins to feel desperate.

The distractions can come in the form of discouragement,
accusations, oppression, depression, or any other fruitless attempt
to prevent the will of the Father from being birthed.

Distract is defined as "to draw away or divert, as the mind or
attention; to disturb or trouble greatly in mind; beset." The enemy

always wants your attention to be on him and not on God. He wants to draw you away from what the Lord wants you doing, and he wants you to waste your time, your attention, and your energy on fruitless distractions.

Distractions can start with a simple thought or words spoken to you, about you, or by you. Don't get distracted, first and foremost, from the presence of the Lord. When you are in the presence of the Lord, you can clearly hear His direction, and you are reminded of His promises to you.

Luke 10:40 says,

But Martha was distracted by all the preparations that had to be made. She came to him and asked, "Lord, don't you care that my sister has left me to do the work by myself? Tell her to help me!"

Martha was having a pity party, and she was angry at Mary. Martha was all bent out of shape, but the Lord told her Mary had chosen what was better. We aren't supposed to be busy. We are supposed to be fruitful! If the enemy can distract you from your purpose, you will become busy, but remain fruitless.

When the distractions come—because they will come—we must watch our reaction to the distractions. Paul faced many distractions, but he never lost his focus. Paul had the right reaction to the distraction—he just shook it off!

Nehemiah had the right reaction to the distractions of the enemy. He worked with one hand and fought with the other. He prayed to God, he refused to talk to the enemy, and he never lost focus concerning the job God had sent him to do.

When you succumb to the enemy's temptation to try to bring about your own season of suddenlies, suddenly all you have is a big mess! Abraham and Sarah suddenly had an Ishmael to deal with. But when we allow God to control the season of suddenlies in our lives, we are so blessed.

SUDDEN BLESSINGS

After Job prayed for his friends and forgave those who hurt him, the Lord turned things around. The Lord made Job prosperous again and gave him twice as much as he had to begin with (see Job 42:10). Job received double for his trouble because he kept his heart right and he maintained his integrity (see Job 2:3). Even though Job lost it all, the best was yet to come! God turned it around.

For Jesus, turnaround time came at the resurrection. Things looked really bad when they crucified Jesus on the cross, but it wasn't over until it was over. And for you today, it isn't over yet!

Turnaround time is coming for you, too. Father is about to resurrect your dead dreams, revive your lagging visions, and resuscitate your choked-out hopes.

After many years of faithfulness, Joseph was suddenly promoted. After standing their ground against mixture and compromise, Shadrach, Meshach, and Abednego were suddenly promoted. After losing it all, Job suddenly stepped into double blessings.

Although Job and Joseph both went through challenging times, neither one of them ever went back. Neither of them ever had to go through what they went through again. I believe the Lord is saying the same thing for you today—you will never have to go back. You will never again go through what you went through. It's promotion time! Welcome to the season of suddenlies!

DON'T LET DIVINE REARRANGEMENTS BECOME DISAPPOINTMENTS

Although there are no more disappointments in the season of suddenlies, there are rearrangements. Joseph was just entering into his season of suddenlies when his plan or vision appeared to get rearranged. He was in Potiphar's house one day and in the prison the next. Suddenly his plan was rearranged, but it wasn't meant to be a disappointment—in fact, it was meant to be a divine appointment. God was placing and positioning him for the greatest—for the completion and the fulfillment of his dream and vision.

Don't get rearrangements confused with disappointments. Never allow yourself to get disappointed over a God-ordained rearrangement. God knows what He's doing, and it's all good!

Genesis 39:19 says, *"When his master heard the story his wife told him, saying, 'This is how your slave treated me,' he burned with anger."* The Word says his master heard the "story." That's exactly what it was—a story! It wasn't the truth. My grandmother used to always say to us as children, "Don't you tell me a story. You'd better tell me the truth." Potiphar's wife told a "story" about Joseph that contradicted his true character. The truth always comes out, folks! Don't be discouraged when false accusations are spoken against you. Don't retaliate when people tell "stories" about you. God is your defense, and the truth will come out, even if it takes twenty-five years!

> *Joseph's master took him and put him in prison, the place where the king's prisoners were confined. But while Joseph was there in the prison, the Lord was with him; he showed him kindness and granted him favor in the eyes of the prison warden. So the warden put Joseph in charge of all those held in the prison, and he was made responsible for all that was done there. The warden paid no attention to anything under Joseph's care, because the Lord was with Joseph and gave him success in whatever he did* (Genesis 39:20-23).

The Lord was with Joseph, and he was blessed and prosperous. God had a divine rearrangement for Joseph. There was no need for him to feel disappointed or discouraged. God was orchestrating the whole thing. As a matter of fact, God was looking out for Joseph and his best interests. God knew He was setting Joseph up

for greatness, and God is setting you up for greatness today. There will be no more disappointments in this season of suddenlies, so stop expecting them. Start expecting your miracle, start expecting your breakthrough, and start expecting your suddenly!

Turnaround Time Takes You Straight to the Top

Isaiah 49:11 says, *"I will turn all my mountains into roads, and my highways will be raised up."* Don't worry about those mountains—God's about to turn them into a pathway to your palace. Don't worry about those obstacles—God's about to turn them into stepping stones. Don't worry about those false accusations—God is about to use them to supernaturally propel you forward into your purpose. It's turnaround time—get excited!

Isaiah 49:23 says,

Kings will be your foster fathers, and their queens your nursing mothers. They will bow down before you with their faces to the ground; they will lick the dust at your feet. Then you will know that I am the LORD; those who hope in me will not be disappointed.

When your hope is in the Lord, you will never be disappointed because God always turns things around.

Sometimes Things Get Worse Before They Get Better

When God positions you for your turnaround, sometimes things look worse than ever before. Joseph's first stage of the turnaround put him in prison. It's at this stage of the turnaround that

you must hang on to the fact that God is faithful and that He's got your back!

> *Then Nebuchadnezzar was furious with Shadrach, Meshach and Abednego, and his attitude toward them changed. He ordered the furnace heated seven times hotter than usual, and commanded some of the strongest soldiers in his army to tie up Shadrach, Meshach and Abednego and throw them into the blazing furnace* (Daniel 3:19-20).

Have you ever caught yourself saying, "Uh, Lord? This isn't the turnaround that I saw when I was praying. This is not how I pictured it at all! Can we maybe revise the plan, Lord? Please?" Have you ever had someone's attitude toward you totally change overnight? That's what happened with the three Hebrew children. King Nebuchadnezzar's attitude toward them changed, and the blazing furnace was turned up seven times hotter, and then they were thrown in although they were taking a stand for righteousness.

Daniel 3:25 says, *"He said, 'Look! I see four men walking around in the fire, unbound and unharmed, and the fourth looks like a son of the gods.'"* God turned things around for Shadrach, Meshach, and Abednego. When God turns things around, He totally turns things around! They didn't even smell like smoke when they came out of that furnace. It had zero effect on them. Verse 28 says that God sent His angel and rescued Shadrach, Meshach, and Abednego. God has His angels on assignment for your turnaround, as well! God totally turned things around, and then came promotion time.

> *Therefore I decree that the people of any nation or language who say anything against the God of Shadrach, Meshach and Abednego be cut into pieces and their houses be turned into piles of rubble, for no other god can save in this way. Then the king*

promoted Shadrach, Meshach and Abednego in the province of Babylon (Daniel 3:29-30).

God turned the situation around for the three Hebrew boys, and then He supplied supernatural promotion. Promotion always comes from the Lord, and it always comes after turnaround time. Your sudden promotion will always come after your turnaround time, as well!

Maybe you are in a time of turnaround that doesn't look all that exciting. It may seem seven times worse. The false accusations and the disloyalty of those you trusted may be weighing on your heart today. First, make the choice to forgive and release those who have hurt you, and then rejoice—supernatural promotion is just around the corner! Go ahead and shout now: "God is doing a new thing!"

Isaiah 43:18-19 says,

Forget the former things; do not dwell on the past. See, I am doing a new thing! Now it springs up; do you not perceive it? I am making a way in the desert and streams in the wasteland.

As we forget the former things and stop dwelling on the past, we can successfully embrace the new things God has for us. We can successfully embrace the season of suddenlies, which holds so many exciting things in the very near future.

Even if you are let go from your job or you lose your house, who is to say that God isn't positioning you for your turnaround? Things may look seven times worse or seven times hotter than ever before, but God is positioning you for your turnaround, so just hang on for the faith ride.

The Season of Suddenlies Is Payback Time

We can't look to people to repay us for things that we have lost. No one can repay you for the pain you suffered from abuse,

betrayal, or any other loss. When we look to people to repay us, it's called unforgiveness.

When you hold bitterness and anger, you are saying, "You must repay me for my pain or my loss." But the truth is no person can repay you for years you have lost, the pain you have experienced, or the disappointments you have suffered. But God can, and He will.

Joel 2:25 says, *"I will repay you for the years the locusts have eaten."* The truth is, when anything has been stolen from us, the real root lies with the enemy. Satan comes to steal, kill, and destroy, but Jesus came to give us life—life more abundant (see John 10:10). As we understand that our battle is not against flesh and blood, but against principalities and powers of darkness (see Eph. 6:12), we can successfully stop looking to people to repay us in a way that is impossible.

But God tells us in Joel chapter 2 that He will repay us in the areas where we have suffered loss, and I can tell you firsthand— He will do just that!

GET READY FOR YOUR SUDDENLY!

When you are in the season of suddenlies, overnight there is an immediate, smooth transition from the old to the new season. We can't afford to quit until our dreams and visions become a reality. Joseph never quit in pursuing his purpose with a passion. He never gave in to ungodliness. Joseph always did the righteous thing—he maintained his character and integrity and kept his eyes on the finish line. As a result, he was promoted overnight.

The season of suddenlies is what causes you to cross the finish line to your dreams and visions. But when your suddenly arrives, it's important to have a heart that's free of compromise—a heart that, like Joseph's, is marked by Christ-like character and integrity.

You must be dressed and ready for where you are going when your day of suddenly arrives. Joseph was clothed in character, which is much more important than any gift or talent. Joseph's call took him to a place of great authority and power. But he had allowed the Lord to develop his Christian character and his integrity to the point that he was ready for his God-ordained position.

All too often, people's gifts and talents take them to a place that their character can't keep them. They become a shooting star for the Lord, and they just fizzle out due to their lack of character and integrity.

Joseph, on the other hand, was dressed and ready in the natural and in the spirit when his "suddenly" arrived. Genesis 41:14 says, *"So Pharaoh sent for Joseph, and he was quickly brought from the dungeon. When he had shaved and changed his clothes, he came before Pharaoh."*

After Joseph was shaved and ready, he was quickly or suddenly brought before Pharaoh, and thus his dream and vision were fulfilled. God had actually showed Joseph his suddenly from the very beginning.

> *Joseph had a dream, and when he told it to his brothers, they hated him all the more. He said to them, "Listen to this dream I had: We were binding sheaves of grain out in the field when suddenly my sheaf rose and stood upright, while your sheaves gathered around mine and bowed down to it"* (Genesis 37:5-7).

God told Joseph from the very beginning that the fulfillment of his dream would happen "suddenly." I'm sure Joseph was probably a lot like us in the fact that he thought for sure his "suddenly" would happen within thirty days—ninety days, maximum. But that wasn't the timing of God's suddenly. Joseph had to be prepared along the way, but that's like the fine print of a contract—you don't usually find out about that part until you are already committed. God does it that way on purpose!

Finally, Joseph's suddenly arrived, and he was ready and prepared for it. God had positioned and prepared him to be a great success.

How about you? Are you dressed and ready for where you are going? Don't be caught off guard concerning your suddenly. Don't give up hope and miss your suddenly when it does arrive.

I believe you are about to step into your suddenly. So get "shaved and ready" because your suddenly is just around the corner. Allow God to shave off the things of the past. Allow God to shave off the flesh and clothe you with new garments in the spirit. Suddenly God is going to turn everything around for you, like He did for Joseph, and you are going to see the fulfillment of your dreams and visions!

LITTLE KEYS TO ABUNDANT PROVISION

Key #14: Get "shaved and ready" for your suddenly!

QUESTIONS FOR REFLECTION AND PERSONAL APPLICATION

1. How patient are you when it comes to waiting on God? What can you do to improve in this area?

2. Have you ever tried to help God, only to find that you've made a bigger mess of things? What did you take away from that experience?

3. What has been your experience with seasons of "suddenlies"? How has your "suddenly" affected your faith?

4. Think back to a time when things got worse before they improved. How has that experience impacted the way you have faced subsequent problems?

Prayer

Repent of any times you have grown impatient with God or tried to help Him according to your own agenda rather than His. Ask Him to help you to trust in His perfect timing and to be prepared when your suddenly arrives.

CHAPTER 15

"I WILL LIFT YOU UP"

Therefore humble yourselves under the mighty hand of God, that He may exalt you in due time, casting all your care upon Him, for He cares for you.

—1 Peter 5:6-7 NKJV

The way up is often down. To illustrate, I often use an experience I had in my early years of ministry, when the Lord was positioning me to prosper spiritually. He told me to do city-wide crusades in a couple of different locations across the nation, and He said that if I obeyed His voice, I would take a step up in the ministry. Well, I was very excited about taking this step up, and I immediately set out to do what He told me to do. As I did, I faced many little surprises and then one huge surprise. The huge surprise was that my step "up" involved a big step down.

As I prepared for the crusade, I worked with pastors and youth pastors from churches throughout the area where the crusade was to be held. I was surprised to find out that not everyone wanted to work together. And as a matter of fact, *most* of them didn't want to work together! I was in my early twenties, and this came as a great surprise to me. We did have many who chose to work together, and those who were involved made commitments as to what their part would be. They made commitments to give financially and to volunteer for various jobs that were needed before, during, and after the event.

As the big weekend approached, hardly anyone was keeping their commitments, including the volunteer workers. All of a sudden, the promised funds were nowhere to be found. I began to feel overwhelmed, and I wished that I had never made the commitments myself to all of the vendors, especially for the auditoriums and coliseums. That was a lot of money.

After a very disappointing planning meeting just before the scheduled crusade, I flew out to Mississippi to preach at a weekend revival. During the entire flight, the only thing I could think about was the meeting that I had just had. No one had kept his financial commitment, and the payment was almost due. In the midst of my flight, the plane began to shake violently, and everyone on board became a little nervous. I can remember looking out the window, imagining what would happen if the plane crashed. I thought, *Well, Lord, I know that I would go to heaven if this plane crashed, and I know that I wouldn't have to go face all those people I owe money to next week.* I quickly took authority over those thoughts and began to pray.

When we finally landed at the airport, I was surprised to see what they called an "airport" in rural Mississippi. I said to myself, "Is this a joke? Am I on *Candid Camera*?" The entire "airport" was less than a thousand square feet—including the baggage claim! As I entered the airport, I looked around to see if I could find the pastor I was preaching for that weekend. After I spent several minutes trying to find him, I proceeded to the baggage claim area, which was only a hundred feet away, I might add. I thought to myself, *This just keeps getting better!* The baggage claim reminded me of an

oversized bread box. I stood with a small group of people, all of us waiting for the metal box lid to be raised so we could get our luggage. Moments later, a single individual rolled back the "bread-box lid," lifted out all of the luggage, and then lowered the lid again by hand. Again, I said to myself, This must be *Candid Camera!* I knew I should laugh, but I wanted to cry. I couldn't believe it. Was this a part of my "step up"? I was excited to be flying to my meeting. After all, most of the time back then, I was still driving to my meetings, even when they were all the way across the country.

I looked once more around the thousand-square-foot airport in an attempt to find the pastor who was supposed to pick me up. Not seeing him, I reached into my pocket and pulled out 52 cents—my entire travel budget for the trip. I didn't even have a cell phone back then, so I went to the pay phone and put in my travel money to call him. And I got his answering machine. Now I was traveling with only 27 cents to my name! When I hung up the receiver, I turned around and heard my name being called by the travel agent at the ticket counter.

He said, "Are you Danette?"

I responded, "Yes."

He said, "The pastor who was supposed to pick you up tonight just called and said he forgot you were coming. He and his wife went to a Kenneth Copeland meeting."

Forgot me? I thought. *I'm the guest speaker! I mean, I know I'm not Kenneth or Gloria Copeland, but how could you forget me?* By this time, I was getting a little ticked off.

And then the guy at the ticket counter said, "I told the pastor that I wouldn't mind taking you to a local hotel."

I bet you wouldn't! I thought. I didn't know this guy, and I wasn't going to let him take me to any hotel! I couldn't believe the day I was having. It had started out bad, with all of the broken

237

promises at my planning meeting, and now it was ending on an even worse note. I was thirsty, so I went to the vending machine to get a drink, only to realize I didn't even have enough change for even one soda.

Needless to say, I gave the guy at the ticket counter quite the interrogation. After I finished my round of twenty questions, I felt really bad. He was a very nice Christian young man who really loved God. The pastor had called the hotel and made arrangements to pay for my room. This young man helped me with my luggage and took me to the hotel.

When I finally got to my room, I put my bags down, plopped onto the bed, looked up at the ceiling, and said, "Lord, this wasn't my idea to do these crusades. This was Your idea, and You said that if I obeyed, I would take a step up." I went on to say, "Don't look now, Lord, but this is hardly a step up!" I had never spoken to the Lord that way before.

Neither have I forgotten His immediate reply: "What goes up must come down. And the farther you are going to go up, the farther you must come down!"

Wow! The way up really is down, and God was teaching me this biblical principle at a young age. The more we are going to do for the Lord—the higher we are going to go in Him—the farther *down* we must go in dying to our flesh and our pride. God went on to teach me that pride is a defense of insecurity. When we are insecure, as I was then, we often rely on pride as a defense to disguise our insecurity to others—even to ourselves. I quickly learned that no one can take pride to the palace—no one!

As we set out to come into our purpose in God, He strategically positions us so that He can prepare us for our "palace" destination. Like Joseph, I was being prepared by God as He challenged me to grow in my character, to die to my flesh, and to put any and all pride out of my life.

Genesis 37:28 says,

So when the Midianite merchants came by, his brothers pulled Joseph up out of the cistern and sold him for twenty shekels of silver to the Ishmaelites, who took him to Egypt.

It didn't look good for Joseph in the natural. It looked like he had lost everything. But in reality, the Ishmaelites took him straight to his destiny! God was still positioning him for the palace. He was stripped of everything, thrown into a pit, and then sold into slavery, but God knew what He was doing!

And God knows what He's doing in your life today. If you stop focusing so much on where you are, you can start focusing on where you are going—the palace! God is positioning you because of your potential. The preparation for the palace comes to a screeching halt if you allow bitterness, resentment, or anger to come into your heart during the positioning process.

When I was doing those crusades and traveling to Mississippi, it wasn't the people around me who were the problem—it was me. And God used those experiences to teach me about myself and to prepare me for my destiny. Preparation always entails character growth, because while we are interested in where we are going, God is more interested in *who* we are when we get there! I couldn't take my pride to the palace, and God lovingly sent me a few pits to take care of the problem.

CONDITIONS FOR MIRACULOUS SUSTENANCE

In First Kings 17, it is recorded that the nation of Israel came under judgment because of King Ahab's promotion of Baal worship. Israel was in a crisis, and God sent Elijah as His representative. The drought they faced was divine judgment on a nation that had turned to idolatry, and it was a demonstration that Baal was powerless to give rain, even though he was their "god of the rain clouds."

> *Now Elijah the Tishbite, from Tishbe in Gilead, said to Ahab, "As the LORD, the God of Israel, lives, who I serve, there will be neither dew nor rain in the next few years except at my word." Then the word of the LORD came to Elijah: "Leave here, turn eastward and hide in the Kerith Ravine, east of the Jordan. You will drink from the brook, and I have ordered the ravens to feed you there"* (1 Kings 17:1-4).

HUMBLE OBEDIENCE

It's so important to hear the Word of the Lord and immediately obey what He says. God told Elijah to leave, and when he did, so did the blessing of the Lord. The people of the land were left isolated from God's Word and His blessings.

But God kept Elijah hidden during those difficult times, and He does the same thing for us. Even though our nation and the world may be going through a drought financially, even though others may be suffering the consequences of their idol worship (material things), God keeps us hidden in His presence, and He always provides for us.

God supernaturally made provisions for Elijah, whose immediate steps of obedience caused those provisions to cross his path. God's provision is always at His place of positioning—we just need to obey His voice and be where we are supposed to be when we are supposed to be there!

HUMBLE GRATITUDE FOR "MANNA"

During these times—drinking from the brook and eating raven food—we may be tempted to complain about the manna. I

will encourage you with something the Lord spoke to me during my "corn dog" years—"You will have to decline to whine while you dine." In other words, be quiet and stop complaining about the manna that God has provided for you. When I would get tired of corn dogs and when I started to complain about God's provision, He would tell me to fast. After a twenty-one-day fast, those corn dogs tasted like filet mignon, and I couldn't wait to eat one.

God has a sense of humor, and if need be, He will get us into a position where we decline to whine about the provision and we get shouting happy about a corn dog!

I can imagine that it must have been a little humbling to the prophet to be drinking from a brook and eating raven food. Sometimes our pride causes us to miss the miracle that's in the manna. Instead of rejoicing over the miracle, we are found whining about the circumstances. Pride is usually at the root of such whining. Pride is usually a defense of insecurity, but when you know who you are in Christ, when your identity and security are in Him, you can rejoice at the miracle in the manna, and you can even enjoy your dining without any whining!

HUMBLE FAITHFULNESS

Elijah was a faithful servant, and God miraculously sustained him. It always pays to be faithful. During financial difficulties, we must keep tithing, we must keep walking in obedience, and we must keep giving. Elijah did what the Lord told him to do, and his obedience brought him into great success.

In those days, only kings ate meat on a daily basis. Common, ordinary people did not. Yet, in the midst of the famine, in the midst of the drought, God fed the man of God like a king! First Kings 17:6 says, *"The ravens brought him bread and meat in the morning and bread and meat in the evening, and he drank from the*

241

brook." That's awesome—Elijah ate like a king once he declined to whine and he walked in obedience to the Word of the Lord.

As I mentioned before, I'm sure it was quite an adjustment for Elijah to be getting his provision from a brook and a flock of ravens. Yet God saw fit to take him "down" another notch so to speak when the brook dried up. I have learned to rejoice when things look like they are taking me "down" because what goes up in God must first go down. And the farther you are going to go up in God, the farther you must go down. The more we are humbled, the more of the power of God can flow through us. The less our flesh glories, the more the glory of the Lord can shine through us.

HUMBLED BY THE BROOK GOING DRY

First Kings 17:7 says, *"Some time later the brook dried up because there had been no rain in the land."* "Some time" later—in other words, in the next season, or phase, of God's plan for Elijah's life. Usually, when "some time later" arrives in my life, I'm just starting to adjust to the new season. Like many of you, I love the familiar. I don't see why we should change anything unless it really, really needs to be changed. I like having the same staff person in the same position year after year. I like sitting in the same seat at church every time I go. I even like having the same hairstyle for as long as possible because I get used to things and don't want them to change.

Even though God is the same yesterday, today, and forever (see Heb. 13:8), He often sees fit to change our situations and circumstances on a regular basis. I believe a part of these changes are to humble us and to get us to be 100 percent dependent on Him. He wants us to be dependent on Him for our provision and not on a paycheck, a boss, a job, and not even a brook! He wants us dependent on Him. And He wants our identity and our security to come

from Him, not a position, a title, a portfolio, and not even from a flock of ravens! Only Him!

When the brook dried up, Elijah's source of provision was gone, but it wasn't because he had done anything wrong. It's during times like these that the enemy tries to condemn us and accuse us. The Word says that there is no condemnation to those who are in Christ (see Rom. 8:1). Don't fall for the scheme of the enemy and think God is judging you or punishing you by causing your source of provision to run dry. Most likely, God is setting you up to take you up. He wants to humble you in order to take you up a notch in your faith. He wants you take your higher in your hope and trust in Him.

HUMBLED BY A SHIFT IN ASSIGNMENTS

When you want to be used by God, you must be flexible with a capital "F." When you are flexible, you bend. But when you aren't flexible, you can easily break. Yes, God wants to often break our will so we learn obedience and trust, but He never wants to break our spirits. Be flexible and welcome your new assignment—God has need of you at another place! You may be the key to someone else's miracle, just as Elijah was the key to the widow woman's miracle. God changed his assignment in order to bring the widow's miracle.

If you recently lost your job, it's possible that you fulfilled your God-given assignment in that role, and now God wants to lead you somewhere else. If you lost your house, I believe God has a divine appointment for you in another neighborhood. Remember, God is in control, even when it doesn't look like it.

The brook that had been Elijah's provision dried up because of what was happening in the land. There was a famine in the land due to the nation's worship of idols and their turning away from God. But for Elijah and the others whose hearts remained pure

243

before the Lord, God continued to hide them and miraculously provide for them.

However, Elijah's assignment changed. First Kings 17:8-9 says, *"Then the word of the LORD came to him; 'Go at once to Zarephath of Sidon and stay there. I have commanded a widow in that place to supply you with food.'"* Elijah received some new marching orders that made it look as if he was being "downsized." Once again, God was messing with his comfort zone! But it was because God wanted to bring Elijah to a new level. Elijah was faced with a challenge to pass the trust test, the change test, and the dreaded obedience test. Yet all along, God was trying to get Elijah out of his comfort zone in order to bring him into his potential zone.

God had brought Elijah through before, and He was going to bring him through again. And He will do the same for you. Stop and think about it. Has God ever not come through for you? Have you ever starved to death? Have you even perished due to a lack of a roof over your head? Of course not, or you wouldn't be reading this book right now. So bring things into perspective—God is still on the throne. Maybe your brook has dried up, but your God hasn't! He's just cheering you on to the next level!

> *"As surely as the LORD your God lives," she replied, "I don't have any bread—only a handful of flour in a jar and a little oil in a jug. I am gathering a few sticks to take home and make a meal from myself and my son, that we may eat it—and die." Elijah said to her, "Don't be afraid. Go home and do as you have said. But first make a small cake of bread for me from what you have and bring it to me, and then make something for yourself and your son. For this is what the LORD, the God of Israel says: 'The jar of flour will not be used up and the jug of oil will not run dry until the day the LORD gives rain on the land'"* (1 Kings 17:12-14).

244

The widow woman was looking at what she didn't have instead of acknowledging what she did have. She was focused on the fact that she didn't have any bread. But she wasn't focused on the fact that she had all the raw ingredients that she needed in order to get some bread. You may not have all the bread or the money that you need, and you're probably feeling pretty humble. But if you have all the raw ingredients—faith, hope, and your great *big* God—in the mix, you will have all the bread, or money, you need to last a lifetime!

HUMBLED THROUGH DISORIENTATION

After leaving the place he was familiar with and being sustained by the brook and the raven, Elijah experienced another season of what seemed to be another "downsizing"—another challenge to get out of his comfort zone. If you remember, the brook dried up, and God sent him to another unfamiliar place, but promised his needs would be met through a widow he had never met. Imagine it! I don't know about you, but I would probably be in meltdown mode about then!

Just as Elijah was adjusting to one change, then came another one! But Elijah's obedience and his flexibility to God's leading prepared him and qualified him for what God wanted to use him for. Not only was Elijah used to usher in the miracle for the widow woman, but God used Elijah for the entire nation. Elijah called on the name of the Lord his God, and He answered by fire. The fire of God fell on Mount Carmel, and all the people cried out, *"The LORD—he is God!"* (1 Kings 18:39).

When God allows "downsizing" events in our lives, chances are, He is preparing us for a big "upsizing"—an "upsizing" of our faith, our trust, our responsibilities, and our blessings from Him. I always say, "Faith up, don't freak out"—God is only trying to supersize your faith!

245

Little Keys to Abundant Provision

Key #15: Humble yourself, and God will lift you up.

Questions for Reflection and Personal Application

1. Think back to a time when your ego was injured because of the way someone treated you. Have you forgiven that person?

2. How do you typically react to being made inferior? What does God have to say about that?

3. Have you ever had an experience similar to Elijah's, in which your "brook" dried up and you were disoriented by a rearrangement? What was the outcome? How did it affect your relationship with God?

Prayer

Repent of any attitudes of pride and self-exaltation. Humbly acknowledge your dependence on God for provision and commit to living humbly as you await promotion from Him.

A NEW DAY IS DAWNING

Whenever we perceive that we're lacking something, whether it's tangible or not, we tend to think, *If only I had _____, I would be completely satisfied.* It's really not true. *If only I were rich* is a common sentiment. So is *If only I were married,* or *If only I hadn't married the wrong person and were still single.* Thoughts such as these enter our minds when we leave them idle—in other words, easily accessed by the enemy. Don't dwell on a perceived lack in any area, for true satisfaction comes only from a relationship with our heavenly Father. I'll say it again: Nothing truly satisfies us except the presence of the Lord. You can have every other desire fulfilled, yet you will still feel unsatisfied if you aren't being "filled" with God's presence on a regular basis.

We are filled with God's presence when we worship Him, pray to Him, and meditate on His Word. And the anointing of the Lord is hidden in His presence. As we spend time in the Father's presence, the anointing on us grows—what could be better than that?

In the night I dreamed that I sought the one whom I love. [She said] I looked for him but could not find him. So I decided to go out into the city, into the streets and broad ways [which are so confusing to a country girl], and seek him whom my soul loves. I sought him, but I could not find him. The watchmen who go about the city found me, to whom I said, Have you seen him who my soul loves? I had gone but a little way past them when I found him whom my soul loves, I held him and would not let him go until I had brought him into my mother's house, and into the chamber of her who conceived me (Song of Solomon 3:1-4 AMP).

In this day and age, we must work hard not to forsake *"him who [our] soul loves."* We must turn off all electronics and communicate! First and foremost, we must communicate with God—daily! And then, we must communicate with those around us. My rule of thumb is, if you can't call, then you can send a text message. But if you can call, do it!

God wants us to want Him, to love Him, and to seek Him above anything else, including financial provision. He has said, *"You will seek me and find me when you seek me with all your heart"* (Jer. 29:13). We have to be determined that we will do whatever it takes to seek Him, and when we find Him, we never let Him go!

[For my determined purpose is] that I may know Him [that I may progressively become more deeply and intimately acquainted with Him, perceiving and recognizing and understanding the wonders of His Person more strongly and more clearly], and that I may in that same way come to know the power outflowing from His resurrection [which it exerts over believers], and that I may so share His sufferings as to be continually transformed [in spirit into His likeness even] to His death... (Philippians 3:10 AMP).

God wants us to strive to *"progressively become more deeply and intimately acquainted with Him."* And we do this primarily

through prayer. Don't wait until you're in the midst of a storm to pray; pray as a daily expression of love for the Lord.

My teenage daughter doesn't shower me with hugs and kisses like she did when she was a toddler—unless she needs something from me or wants me to take her shopping. Unfortunately, that's how we are with God all too often.

Press, Don't Push

Remember, if you are determined to "push" your way, you may get to where you're trying to go—but once you get there, you'll probably wish you hadn't! This is true especially when you make a purchase that requires taking on debt. Instead of pushing your way into debt, press your way into the presence of the Lord and trust Him to meet your needs.

> *Jesus...came to a village where a woman named Martha opened her home to him. She had a sister called Mary, who sat at the Lord's feet listening to what he said. But Martha was distracted by all the preparations that had to be made. She came to him and asked, "Lord, don't you care that my sister has left me to do the work by myself? Tell her to help me!" "Martha, Martha," the Lord answered, "you are worried and upset about many things, but only one thing is needed. Mary has chosen what is better, and it will not be taken away from her"* (Luke 10:38-42).

Unbelievable! Martha had the nerve to tell Jesus that He should command her sister to stop what she was doing—sitting at the feet of Jesus—and join her in her mess of busyness. When we "push" the Lord to give us what we want, when we want it, and how we want it, we shouldn't expect to be blessed.

Choose *"what is better"*—choose to press your way into the Lord's presence and sit at the feet of Jesus every day. Then you will be prepared and equipped to handle whatever season you find yourself in. When we've been at Jesus' feet, everything else falls into place as it should. No matter what we're facing, the presence and anointing of God is all that we need. *"Seek first his kingdom and his righteousness, and all these things will be given to you as well"* (Matt. 6:33).

Jesus told Martha that Mary had chosen what was better, which *"will not be taken away from her."* When we seek the Lord's presence and hang on to His promises, nothing can take that away from us. Situations, circumstances, distractions—none of it can take away what we receive from sitting at His feet!

Press Your Way into a New Day

As we take our position and stand—as we refuse to quit or give up—we press our way to the new day that the Lord has for us. A trick and scheme of the enemy has always been to intimidate, to lie to you and say, "It isn't going to get better. You might as well quit and give up now." But the truth is, just keep pressing your way. Don't push your way, but press your way to the new day.

As we press in through prayer and fasting, we will reach the new day. At midnight, things look dark. At midnight, you can't see things really clear. At midnight, it's still the old day, but at 12:01 A.M., it's a new day! Things may still look the same, but you know it's a new day because the clock tells you it is!

It's the same way with our new day in the Lord. Things may not look any different in the natural. Things may still look like they did at 11:59 P.M., but things are different—it's a brand-new day. You can't tell in the natural that it's a new day for several more hours. But it's a new day, just the same. Before long, that sun starts to rise. Before long, the birds start to chirp. Before long, the rays of sunshine start breaking up the darkness that ruled the sky.

250

And the same is true in the spirit. If you press your way, you will reach the new day that the Lord has for you. Things won't always be the way they are now. Things won't always be the way they have been. You are about to penetrate the new day; you just need to keep pressing your way.

And after you have passed through the midnight hour, after you have entered into the new day, don't be discouraged if things don't look any different at first. You know that it's a new day. You can sense it in your spirit, even though your natural circumstances look the same. Don't let the enemy lie to you—it is a new day. The sun is about to shine again. The darkness is about to be swallowed up by the light. Be encouraged and keep pressing your way!

As you continue to press through financial struggles, as you continue to press your way to the new day in your relationships and in your health, and you continue to press through financial storms that are threatening to tip your boat over, you will come to the new day.

I believe, for many of you, you are just past the midnight hour. It's a new day, but you are tempted to get discouraged because it looks dark, just like the old day. Be encouraged—the Son is about to shine on you. The Lord is about to break up the darkness, and the blessings of the Lord are about to shine through your season of financial darkness. Get ready—the Son is about to rise on your new day!

AUTHOR CONTACT INFORMATION

Joy Ministries

P.O. Box 65036
Virginia Beach, VA 23467

757-420-2625

Joy@JoyMinistriesonline.org

www.JoyMinistries.tv

OTHER BOOKS BY
DANETTE JOY CRAWFORD

Don't Quit in the Pit
Pathway to the Palace